Culinary Arts Institute

PARTIES
for all seasons

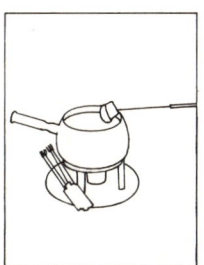

Featured in cover photo:
Chocolate Fondue, page 30

PARTIES

PARTIES FOR ALL SEASONS
**Barbara MacDonald
and the Culinary Arts Institute Staff:**

Helen Geist: Director
Sherrill Corley: Editor • Ethel La Roche: Editorial Assistant
Ivanka Simatic: Recipe Tester
Edward Finnegan: Executive Editor
Charles Bozett: Art Director • John Mahalek: Art Assembly

Book designed and illustrated by Laurel DiGangi

for all seasons

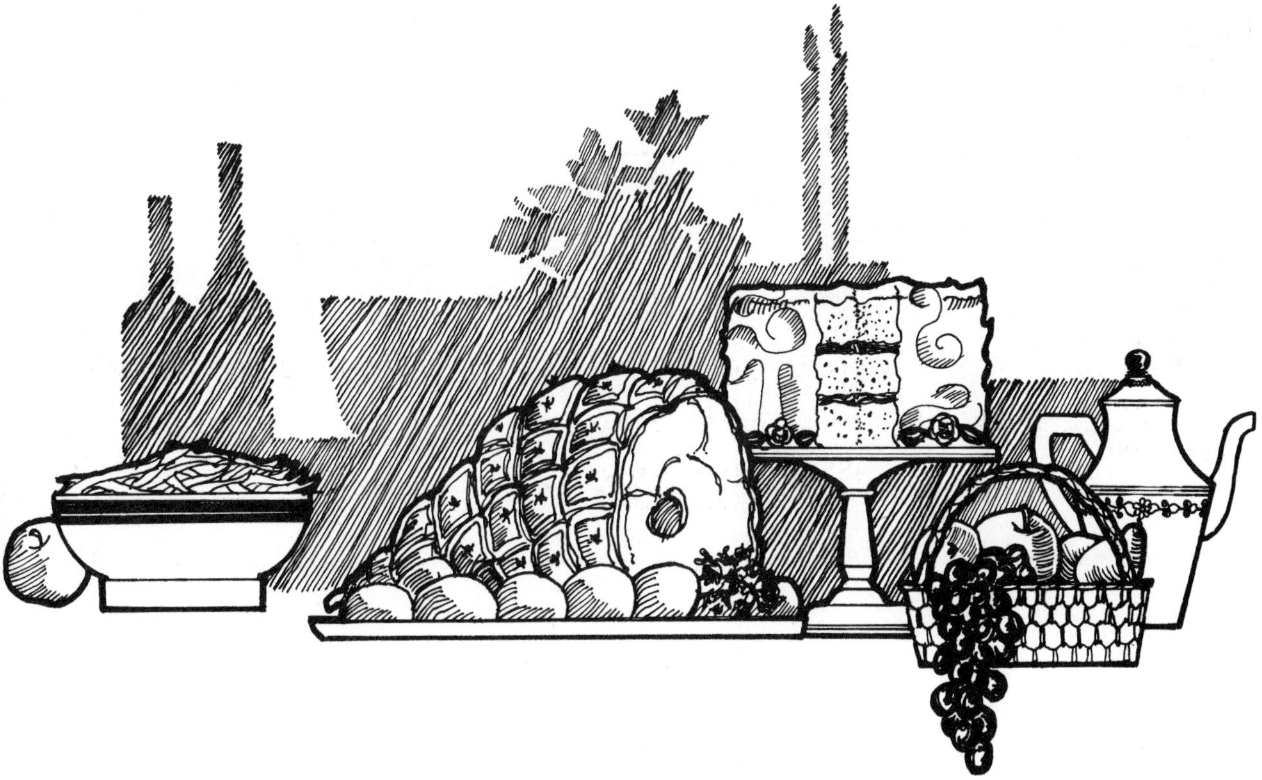

Culinary Arts Institute
1727 South Indiana Avenue, Chicago, Illinois 60616

Copyright © 1976
by
Consolidated Book Publishers

All rights reserved under the International and Pan-American Copyright Conventions. Manufactured in the United States of America and published simultaneously in Canada by Nelson, Foster & Scott, Ltd., Willowdale, Ontario

Library of Congress Catalog Card Number: 75-34804
International Standard Book Number: 0-8326-0549-2

ACKNOWLEDGMENTS
American Mushroom Institute; California Wine Institute;
Diamond Walnut Growers, Inc.; Fresh Bartlett Promotion Advisory Board;
Idaho Oregon Sweet Spanish Onion Promotion Committee;
Nectarine Administrative Committee; North American Blueberry Council;
Union Carbide Corporation Food Science Institute

FOREWORD

Now is the time for all good men—women, and children—to come to the aid of the party! Be it a full-dress lunch or bachelor brunch—youngster's birthday or oldster's retirement—any party will benefit from the thought you give it in advance.

Collected here are enough party ideas to fill your calendar from Ringing in the New Year to the next Hanging Out of Greens.

Get the new year off to a happy start with an open house. A sideboard spread with make-ahead, help-yourself dishes will serve a crowd over an indefinite stretch of afternoon or evening. Cap it off with a handsome dessert for an unforgettable day of "auld lang syne."

Turn the page to February and a host of party possibilities. If your family roster doesn't include a February birthday, borrow one from those famous presidents or let Valentine's Day provide your party theme. Such a party is made to order for the youngsters when the weather favors indoor over outdoor play. For a month that is short on days, February is long on party material.

But don't overlook the grownups in your party plans. If a full-scale dinner party sounds like too much work, enlist a few friends and have a progressive party in March. Start with appetizers at one house and change locale for each of the remaining courses. Everybody shares the work—and the fun.

The party giver isn't strictly feminine in gender. Come April, a young man's thoughts could as easily turn to food as to romance. And if making an impression on a young lady or two is on his mind, he could hardly do better than to invite a crowd for brunch. This abbreviated meal lets him score an entertaining triumph in the smallest possible number of courses.

May arrives, a popular time for bridal showers. While there is no longer a special month for weddings, spring still seems the most romantic season, and showers are perfectly apropos. If you're the hostess, start preparations early and stock the freezer with party-fancy dishes. Or recruit friends to contribute to a salad buffet.

In June the party scene shifts out of doors. The time is ripe for an Ice Cream Social. It's an idea that seems to have gone out with highbutton shoes, but it deserves a comeback. It's one party that knows no age barriers.

In July, A Yankee dude'll have a dandy time cooking up nothing fancier than a grilled hamburger. But you can inspire him to higher achievement with our cookout recipes and party ideas.

In August, the appeal of a picnic is directly

proportional to the rising mercury. Most outdoor meals will be impromptu, but treat yourself to one incredibly elegant picnic—complete with table finery and gourmet food. Perhaps you'll have weekend guests; time your posh picnic to their visit. Have an alfresco wine-tasting while getting your picnic on the table.

In some ways September is the beginning of a new year. It introduces the new session at school, and it's time for Dad's poker club and Mom's bridge group to get under way again. Food is an expected part of such get-togethers, so capitalize on the fresh flavor of fall fruits to prepare a memorable dessert when the party is at your house.

Plenty of action—that's what teenagers like at parties. October's the time for after-the-game and Halloween parties so let the teens plan their own. It means less work for Mom and more fun for them. Food can be the pitch-in-and-do-your-own kind, such as pizza with pizzazz or tacos with a new twist.

November is the traditional time to remember pioneer ancestors through the Thanksgiving feast. It's a good time to remember our real forebears too, with a "come as your ancestor" potluck party. While our first allegiance is to the red, white, and blue, most of us feel a second stirring of pride for the "old sod." Invite your guests to dress in costume and bring a dish reminiscent of the land nourishing the roots of their family tree.

December brings us full circle to the holidays. Tree trimmings, caroling, and winter sports are all more fun when you do them with a party. It's a time when the party giver needs to budget resources—time, money, and work—carefully. During this busy season party know-how pays its biggest dividends.

Good parties don't just happen. Advance planning and pre-party preparation are essential. But they'll develop more easily with the special helps and planning guides offered here—all designed to come to the aid of your party.

CONTENTS

January—Open House 9
Invitations • What to Serve • Decorations
    Beverages   10
    Appetizers   11
    Meat Dishes   13
    Vegetables   14
    Salad Molds   15
    Dessert   16
February—Children's Parties   17
Parties for Preschoolers • Parties for Grade Schoolers
    Train Party for Preschoolers   19
    Grade Schoolers' Valentine Party   20
    Other Choices for Children's Parties   22
March—Progressive Dinner Party   23
How to Organize a Progressive Dinner Party
    Appetizers   24
    Greek Dinner   26
    Continental Cuisine   27
    French Dinner   28
    Desserts   29
April—Bachelor's Brunch   31
Invitations • The Menu
    Gerry's Brunch   32
    Spring Tonic Brunch   34

    Brunch, Bachelor Style 35
May—Bridal Showers 37
Guest List • Invitations • Menu • Activities
    Recipes for a Bridal Shower 38
June—Ice Cream Social 45
The Menu • Making Ice Cream
   Ice Cream 46
   Cakes 49
   Ice Cream Sauces 51
July—Cookout 53
Food • Decorations • Getting Ready to Barbecue
    Main Dishes from the Grill 54
    Sauces and Accompaniments 55
    Barbecue Basics 56
    Side Dishes from the Grill 58
August—Posh Picnics 61
The Menu • The Table Setting • Timing
    Wine Tasting Picnic 62
    Before the Concert Affair 64
    Midsummer Night Scene 66
September—Card Parties 67
Male Call Card Party • Ladies' Night Out •
Mixed Couples' Card Party
    Male Call Card Party 68
    Ladies' Night Out 69
    Mixed Couples' Card Party 71
October—Teen Party 73
Activities • The Food
    Recipes for a Teen Party 74
November—Melting Potluck 79
Planning the Food • Planning Decorations •
Giving the Party
    Traditional Thanksgiving Dinner 80
    Melting Potluck Dinner Party 82
December—Holiday Parties 87
Food • Decorations
   Beverages 88
   Fruitcakes 90
   Cookies 92
   Candy 93
Index 94

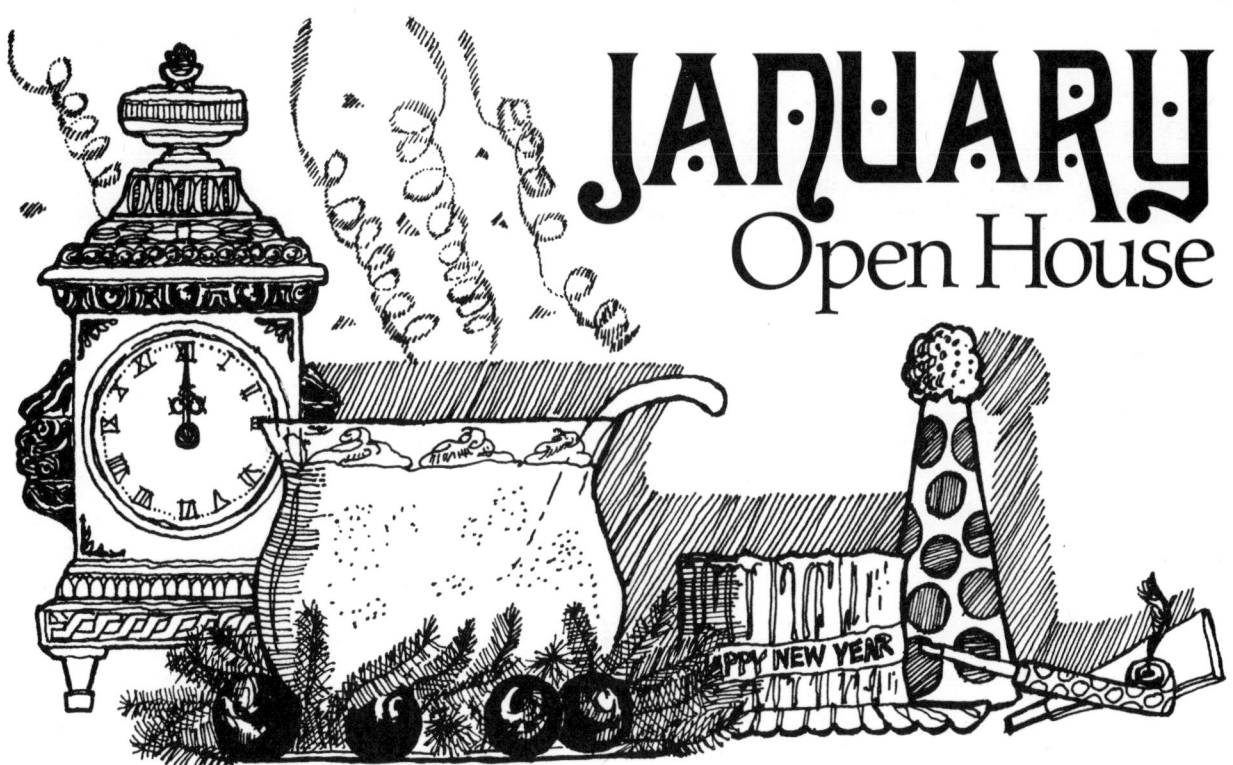

JANUARY Open House

"What are you doing New Year's?"

That question must be as old as Father Time, the bearded gentleman whose exit and reentry we celebrate as the calendar moves ahead. And the question comes naturally. We seem to welcome the chance to give the old year a special send-off and punch the time clock for the one just chiming in.

Should auld acquaintances be forgot? Of course not; old friends should head the guest list for a New Year's party. But remember the newcomers, too, and invite new neighbors and coworkers. Make them feel at home, and in future years you'll have more names to add to the "auld acquaintances."

Some party givers prefer to entertain on New Year's Day rather than New Year's Eve. A January First get-together is a good hedge against that next-day let-down, and there is no compulsion to linger past midnight.

INVITATIONS

Since holidays are busy days, plan to get your invitations out early for a New Year's Open House. Right after Thanksgiving is a good time, before the mails become clogged with the Christmas rush. You can buy ready-made invitations to suit any theme you have in mind, or you can write brief notes on stationery. Something as simple as this is enough:

NEW YEAR'S OPEN HOUSE

January 1

3 P.M. to 7 P.M.

740 S. Main Street

John and Helen Jones

Telephone 123-4567—Regrets Only

The "regrets only" is less stilted than the old fashioned "R.S.V.P." and eliminates calls from the majority—the ones who plan to come.

How many to invite? An open house is an on-the-feet affair; no need to limit yourself to available seating space. Some party veterans recommend inviting 10 percent over the number you hope will come. Allowing for those who won't be able to come, you will still be assured of a good turnout.

WHAT TO SERVE

Do-ahead and delicious—those are requirements for any party food, but they're downright essential at this busy season. You'll probably start thinking about your New Year party in the fall, and you'll be wise to turn those thoughts to action by storing away most of your party menu in the

JANUARY—OPEN HOUSE

freezer as spare hours present themselves.

Finger foods, tidbits to accompany a cup of punch, are well suited to a standup party. Such items as pâté and an eggplant caviar can be done ahead and frozen. And so can a Mushroom Cheese Mold, although purists don't recommend freezing cheese. In this case, the benefits to be gained from advance preparation outweigh the finer points of cheese perfection.

If your open house will stretch from afternoon on through the evening, you may wish to serve something more substantial than appetizers. Late in the day, a tray of cold ham or turkey or a baked casserole such as turkey lasagne would be welcome. In such fancy dress, who will guess they are leftovers from a holiday meal? Accompany the meat with a hot vegetable casserole. A salad mold, or perhaps two, will add frosty beauty to the menu.

Dessert could be Christmas cookies (you're sure to have lots on hand), that fruitcake you received from Uncle George, or a plum pudding you made much earlier in the season.

DECORATIONS

One of the nice things about a New Year's party is the fact that your decorating has already been done as part of your regular seasonal preparations. You're sure to have those holiday items you cherish most out where they can be seen and enjoyed.

BEVERAGES

Champagne Punch

Ice Ring
3 jiggers brandy
3 jiggers curaçao
1 quart chilled champagne
1 quart sparkling water

1. At serving time, turn ice ring into punch bowl.
2. Add brandy, curaçao, champagne, and sparkling water. Serve in punch cups.

About 2 quarts punch

Ice Ring: Fill a ring mold with water and freeze the night before the party. If desired, arrange mint leaves and maraschino cherries in mold to form wreath effect.

Gin Punch

1 can (6 ounces) frozen lemonade concentrate
1 can (6 ounces) frozen orange juice concentrate
1 quart gin
1 quart sparkling water
Ice Ring (this page)

1. In 3-quart punch bowl, combine frozen juices. Let soften a few minutes until mushy.
2. Pour in gin and sparkling water; stir well.
3. Carefully add ice ring and serve.

About 2½ quarts punch

Strawberry Punch

2 cans (18 ounces each) unsweetened pineapple juice
1 cup lemon juice
2 packages (16 ounces each) frozen strawberry halves, partially thawed
1 quart ginger ale, chilled
Ice Ring (this page)

1. Combine pineapple juice and lemon juice in punch bowl.
2. Add the strawberries and their syrup; stir to blend thoroughly.
3. Add the chilled ginger ale and blend. Carefully add ice ring; ladle into punch cups and serve immediately.

About 3 quarts punch

APPETIZERS

Mushrooms à la Grecque

- 1 pound fresh mushrooms or 2 cans (6 to 8 ounces each) whole mushrooms
- ⅓ cup olive oil
- ⅓ cup dry white wine or apple juice
- ¼ cup water
- 1 tablespoon lemon juice
- ¾ cup chopped onion
- 1 large clove garlic, minced
- 1½ teaspoons salt
- 1 teaspoon sugar
- ½ teaspoon coriander seed (optional)
- ¼ teaspoon black pepper
- 2 cups carrot chunks
- ½ cup pimento-stuffed olives

1. Rinse, pat dry, and halve fresh mushrooms or drain canned mushrooms; set aside.
2. In a large saucepan combine oil, wine, water, lemon juice, onion, garlic, salt, sugar, coriander, and black pepper. Bring to boiling; add carrots.
3. Cover and simmer for 15 minutes. Add mushrooms and olives. Return to boiling; reduce heat. Cover and simmer for 5 minutes.
4. Chill thoroughly, at least overnight.
5. To serve, thread mushrooms, carrot chunks, and olives on skewers or spoon into a bowl. Serve as hors d'oeuvres.

8 to 10 hors d'oeuvre portions

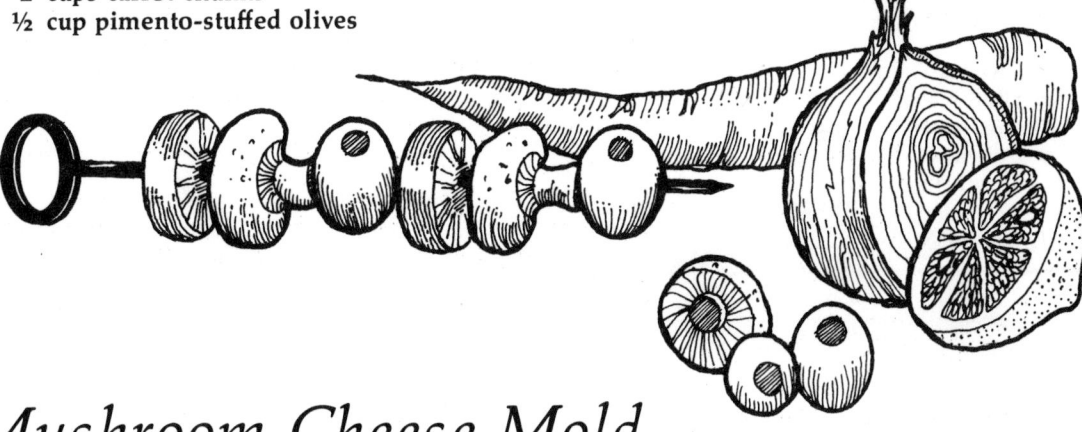

Mushroom Cheese Mold

- 2 packages (8 ounces each) cream cheese, softened
- ½ pound Cheddar cheese, shredded (about 2 cups)
- 1 clove garlic, crushed
- 1½ teaspoons brown mustard
- ¼ teaspoon salt
- 1 can (3 to 4 ounces) mushroom stems and pieces, drained and chopped
- ¼ cup finely chopped onion
- 2 tablespoons finely diced pimento
- 2 tablespoons finely chopped parsley
- Sliced mushrooms (optional)
- Parsley (optional)

1. Combine cheeses, garlic, mustard, and salt in a bowl. Add chopped mushrooms, onion, pimento, and parsley; mix well.
2. Turn mixture into a lightly buttered 3-cup mold. Refrigerate until firm.
3. Unmold onto serving platter. Garnish with sliced mushrooms and parsley, if desired. Serve with **crackers**.

3½ cups spread

Clam and Walnut Stuffed Mushrooms

20 large mushrooms
½ cup butter or margarine
1 clove garlic, minced
1 can (10 ounces) minced or whole baby clams, drained
1 cup soft bread crumbs
½ cup chopped walnuts
¼ cup chopped parsley
¼ teaspoon salt
¼ teaspoon black pepper
Walnut halves (optional)
Parsley sprigs (optional)

1. Rinse mushrooms and pat dry. Remove stems and chop (about 1 cup); set aside.
2. Melt butter in a large skillet. Use about 3 tablespoons of melted butter to brush on mushroom caps. Place caps in a shallow pan.
3. To butter remaining in skillet, add garlic and reserved chopped mushroom stems; sauté 2 minutes. Add clams, bread crumbs, nuts, parsley, salt, and pepper; mix well.
4. Spoon stuffing into mushroom caps, piling high.
5. Bake at 350°F about 12 minutes, or until hot.
6. If desired, garnish with walnut halves and parsley sprigs.

20 stuffed mushrooms

Blue Cheese Dip with Vegetable Strips

½ cup crumbled blue cheese
½ cup dairy sour cream
½ cup mayonnaise
½ cup finely chopped celery
½ teaspoon salt
2 drops Tabasco
Vegetable strips, such as celery green pepper, carrots, or mushrooms

1. Mix cheese, sour cream, mayonnaise, celery, salt, and Tabasco in a bowl. Chill thoroughly.
2. Serve vegetables as dippers.

About 1½ cups dip

Mock Caviar (Eggplant)

1 medium eggplant
1 or 2 medium onions, minced
1 tomato, peeled and minced
1 clove garlic, minced
Salt and pepper to taste
3 tablespoons vinegar
¼ cup olive oil
1 package (8 ounces) cream cheese

1. Pierce skin of eggplant with fork in 3 or 4 places and place whole eggplant in baking dish. Bake at 350°F about 1 hour, or until skin is wrinkled and soft. Remove from oven; plunge into cold water until cool enough to handle. Remove stem and skin; discard. Cut eggplant into pieces; mash pulp and seeds with a fork in mixing bowl. Add onion, tomato, garlic, salt, pepper, vinegar, and oil. Chill.
2. At serving time, unwrap cream cheese and place rectangle on serving plate. Cover with mock caviar and serve as a spread with **crackers, party rye bread,** or **pumpernickel.**

Chicken Liver Pâté

2 tablespoons butter or margarine
½ pound chicken livers
¼ cup chopped onion
¼ cup hot chicken broth
1 tablespoon cognac
1 teaspoon Worcestershire sauce
⅛ teaspoon garlic salt

1. Heat butter in a small skillet; add chicken livers and onion and cook over medium heat until lightly browned, stirring occasionally. Blend in chicken broth; cook over low heat about 5 minutes, or until livers are very tender.
2. Combine in electric blender container cognac, Worcestershire sauce, garlic salt, curry powder, paprika, and pepper. Add livers, about ½ cup at a time, along with liquid in skillet,

JANUARY—OPEN HOUSE 13

¼ teaspoon curry powder
¼ teaspoon paprika
⅛ teaspoon pepper
3 tablespoons butter or margarine, softened

and blend at high speed until mixture is smooth. Beat in the softened butter, a small amount at a time.

3. Turn pâté into bowl and refrigerate until firm. Serve with crisp crackers or small toast triangles.

About ¾ cup pâté

MEAT DISHES

Turkey Lasagne

¼ pound bulk pork sausage, browned
1 can (28 ounces) tomatoes, drained
2 tablespoons chopped parsley
½ teaspoon salt
1 teaspoon crushed basil
1 teaspoon crushed rosemary
1 bay leaf
1 clove garlic, minced
1 to 1½ cups cooked turkey pieces
1½ cups creamed cottage cheese
¼ cup finely chopped parsley
2 eggs, beaten
½ teaspoon seasoned salt
½ teaspoon monosodium glutamate
¼ teaspoon pepper
½ pound lasagne noodles, cooked, drained, and rinsed
½ cup shredded Parmesan cheese
½ pound Swiss cheese, thinly sliced

1. Simmer the sausage, tomatoes, 2 tablespoons parsley, salt, basil, rosemary, bay leaf, and garlic together in an uncovered skillet until thick, about 30 minutes. Remove bay leaf; mix in turkey and heat sauce thoroughly.
2. Meanwhile, mix cottage cheese, ¼ cup parsley, and a blend of beaten eggs and seasonings.
3. Spread one fourth of sauce in a 2-quart shallow casserole. Top with a third of noodles. Using a third of each, spread noodles with cottage cheese mixture, then sprinkle with Parmesan cheese, and arrange Swiss cheese slices on top. Repeat layering and end with sauce.
4. Bake at 350°F about 30 minutes, or until bubbly. Remove from oven and let stand 5 minutes.

8 servings

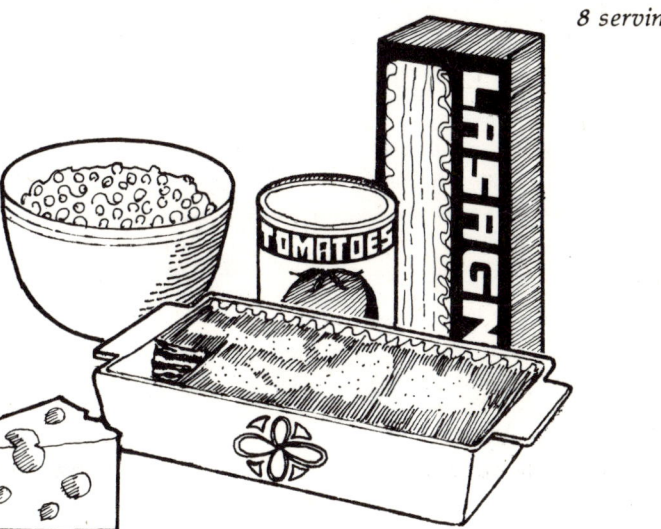

Glazed Smoked Ham

5- to 7-pound fully cooked smoked ham, butt half
½ cup firmly packed brown sugar
2 teaspoons flour
½ teaspoon dry mustard
1 tablespoon cider vinegar

1. Place ham, fat side up, on rack in a shallow roasting pan; insert meat thermometer. Heat uncovered at 325°F until thermometer registers 130°F (allowing 18 to 24 minutes per pound).
2. About 45 minutes before end of heating period, trim and score fat surface of ham to make a diamond pattern. Spread with glazing mixture of brown sugar, flour, dry mustard, and vinegar. Return to oven for about 45 minutes.

VEGETABLES

Herbed Carrots with Grapes

1½ pounds carrots
½ teaspoon salt
1 teaspoon basil
½ cup butter or margarine
1 small clove garlic, minced
½ teaspoon thyme
¼ teaspoon celery salt
1 cup seedless grapes
1 tablespoon lemon juice
⅛ teaspoon salt
Few grains pepper

1. Wash and pare carrots; cut into 3×¼-inch strips. Put into a saucepan; add the ½ teaspoon salt, basil, and enough boiling water to almost cover. Cook covered 12 to 15 minutes, or until carrots are crisp-tender.
2. Meanwhile, melt butter and add garlic, thyme, and celery salt. Set aside.
3. When carrots are cooked, remove from heat immediately. Add grapes and let stand covered 1 to 2 minutes; drain off liquid.
4. Stir lemon juice into garlic butter and pour over hot carrots. Season with salt and pepper; toss mixture gently.

6 to 8 servings

Make-Ahead Mashed Potatoes

5 pounds potatoes
½ cup margarine
2 packages (3 ounces each) cream cheese, softened
1 cup dairy sour cream
4 ounces extra sharp Cheddar cheese, shredded (optional)
½ cup grated Parmesan cheese
4 green onions, chopped
1 tablespoon salt
1 teaspoon pepper

1. Cook potatoes until tender. Mash or rice while hot. Add remaining ingredients and beat well. Turn into a 3-quart casserole. Cover and store in refrigerator up to 2 weeks.
2. On party day, remove casserole from refrigerator 1 hour before baking. If desired, fluff up potatoes with a little **milk**.
3. Bake uncovered at 350°F 45 minutes or until heated through.

10 to 12 servings

Spinach-Cheese Bake

2 packages (10 ounces each) frozen chopped spinach
3 eggs, beaten
¼ cup all-purpose flour
1 teaspoon seasoned salt
¼ teaspoon nutmeg
¼ teaspoon black pepper
2 cups (16 ounces) creamed cottage cheese
2 cups (8 ounces) shredded Swiss or Cheddar cheese

1. Cook spinach following package directions; drain.
2. Combine eggs, flour, seasoned salt, nutmeg, and pepper in a bowl. Mix in cottage cheese, Swiss cheese, and spinach.
3. Turn into a buttered 1½-quart casserole.
4. Bake at 325°F 50 to 60 minutes.

6 to 8 servings

SALAD MOLDS

Overnight Cherry Salad

- 2 cups dairy sour cream
- 2 cups creamed cottage cheese
- 2 cups thawed frozen whipped dessert topping
- 1 package (6 ounces) cherry-flavored gelatin
- 1 can (17 ounces) dark sweet cherries, drained
- 1 cup pecans, coarsely chopped

Combine all ingredients in a large bowl and refrigerate overnight. Be sure you add the flavored gelatin dry.

12 to 16 servings

Note: Other variations may be used in various flavors of gelatin and fruit, such as lemon or lime with pineapple; orange with mandarin oranges; strawberry with frozen strawberries.

Artichoke Mousse

- 6 medium-sized artichokes
- 1 onion, peeled and sliced
- 1 lime, sliced
- 2 stalks celery with leaves, cut in pieces
- 3 tablespoons olive oil
- 1½ teaspoons salt
- ½ cup mayonnaise
- 3 tablespoons lime juice
- 2 teaspoons grated onion
- 1 teaspoon Worcestershire sauce
- 1 teaspoon salt
- Few grains freshly ground black pepper
- 2 envelopes unflavored gelatin
- 1 cup cold water
- ½ cup white grape juice
- 1 cup chilled whipping cream, whipped

1. Remove about 1 inch from tops of artichokes by cutting straight across with a sharp knife. Cut off stems about 1 inch from base; remove and discard lower outside leaves. Rinse and drain.
2. Set the artichokes right-side-up in 1 inch boiling water in a large saucepot. Add sliced onion, lime, celery, oil, and 1½ teaspoons salt. Cook, covered, 1 to 1½ hours, or until artichokes are very tender and a leaf can easily be pulled out. Add more water if necessary during cooking.
3. Drain and cool artichokes. Scrape "meat" from leaves; remove thistle (or fuzzy choke) and discard. Remove heart and combine in an electric blender container with "meat," mayonnaise, lime juice, grated onion, Worcestershire sauce, 1 teaspoon salt, and pepper; blend until smooth. (Or use hand rotary or electric beater to blend.) Set aside.
4. Soften gelatin in cold water in a saucepan. Set over low heat and stir until gelatin is completely dissolved. Remove from heat and stir in the grape juice. Set aside until cold.
5. Place a 1½-quart ring mold in a bowl of ice and water. Coat bottom with a small amount of gelatin. Chill until just set, but not firm. Arrange slivers of **ripe olives, pimentos,** and **green onions** in a floral design on bottom of mold.
6. Gently spoon a small amount of gelatin over the design to hold in place. Chill until layer is set, but not firm.
7. Add remaining gelatin to artichoke mixture; blend well. Chill over ice and water, stirring frequently, until mixture mounds slightly when dropped from a spoon. Fold in the whipped cream. Pour over design in mold and chill until firm.
8. Unmold onto a chilled tray and garnish with **curly endive.** Serve with Cooked Pineapple Salad Dressing (page 16).

About 8 servings

Cooked Pineapple Salad Dressing

½ cup butter or margarine
2 tablespoons flour
2 tablespoons sugar
Few grains salt
1 cup unsweetened pineapple juice
1 egg, slightly beaten
2 tablespoons lemon juice

1. Melt the butter in a heavy saucepan. Blend in flour, sugar, and salt; heat until mixture bubbles.
2. Add pineapple juice gradually, stirring constantly. Bring to boiling; stir and cook 3 minutes.
3. Stir about 3 tablespoons of the hot mixture into the beaten egg. Immediately blend into the mixture in saucepan and cook 3 minutes, stirring constantly.
4. Remove from heat and stir in lemon juice. Cool; chill. Store in a covered jar.

About 1½ cups dressing

DESSERT

Light Plum Pudding

2 cups sifted all-purpose flour
2 cups sugar
2 teaspoons baking soda
1 teaspoon salt
1 teaspoon cinnamon
½ teaspoon mace
¼ teaspoon cloves
1 cup fine dry bread crumbs
2 cups finely shredded raw carrot
2 cups finely shredded raw potato
1 tablespoon grated orange peel
¼ cup melted butter or margarine
1 cup pitted dates, cut in pieces
1 cup golden or dark seedless raisins, rinsed and drained
Hard Sauce

1. Sift flour, sugar, baking soda, salt, and spices together into a large bowl. Add the bread crumbs, carrot, potato, orange peel, and melted butter; mix thoroughly. Blend in dates and raisins.
2. Turn into a well-greased 2-quart mold. Cover tightly with greased cover, or tie on aluminum foil, parchment, or double thickness of waxed paper. Place mold on trivet or rack in a steamer or deep kettle with a tight-fitting cover.
3. Pour in boiling water to no more than one half the height of the mold. Cover steamer, bring water to boiling, and keep boiling at all times. If necessary, add more boiling water during cooking period.
4. Steam the pudding 2 hours, or until a wooden pick inserted in center comes out clean.
5. Remove pudding from steamer and uncover; let stand 10 minutes. Invert onto a warm serving platter.
6. Serve with Hard Sauce.

About 12 servings

Note: If pudding is to be stored and served later, unmold onto a rack and cool thoroughly. Wrap in aluminum foil or return to mold and store in a cool place. Before serving, resteam pudding about 3 hours, or until thoroughly heated.

Hard Sauce: Cream **⅔ cup butter** with **2 teaspoons vanilla extract**. Add **2 cups confectioners' sugar** with a **few grains salt** gradually, beating until fluffy after each addition. Beat in **2 teaspoons cream**. Chill until mixture is stiff enough to force through a pastry bag and tube.

About 1⅓ cups

Mushroom-Cheese Mold; Mushrooms à la Grecque;
Clam and Walnut Stuffed Mushrooms

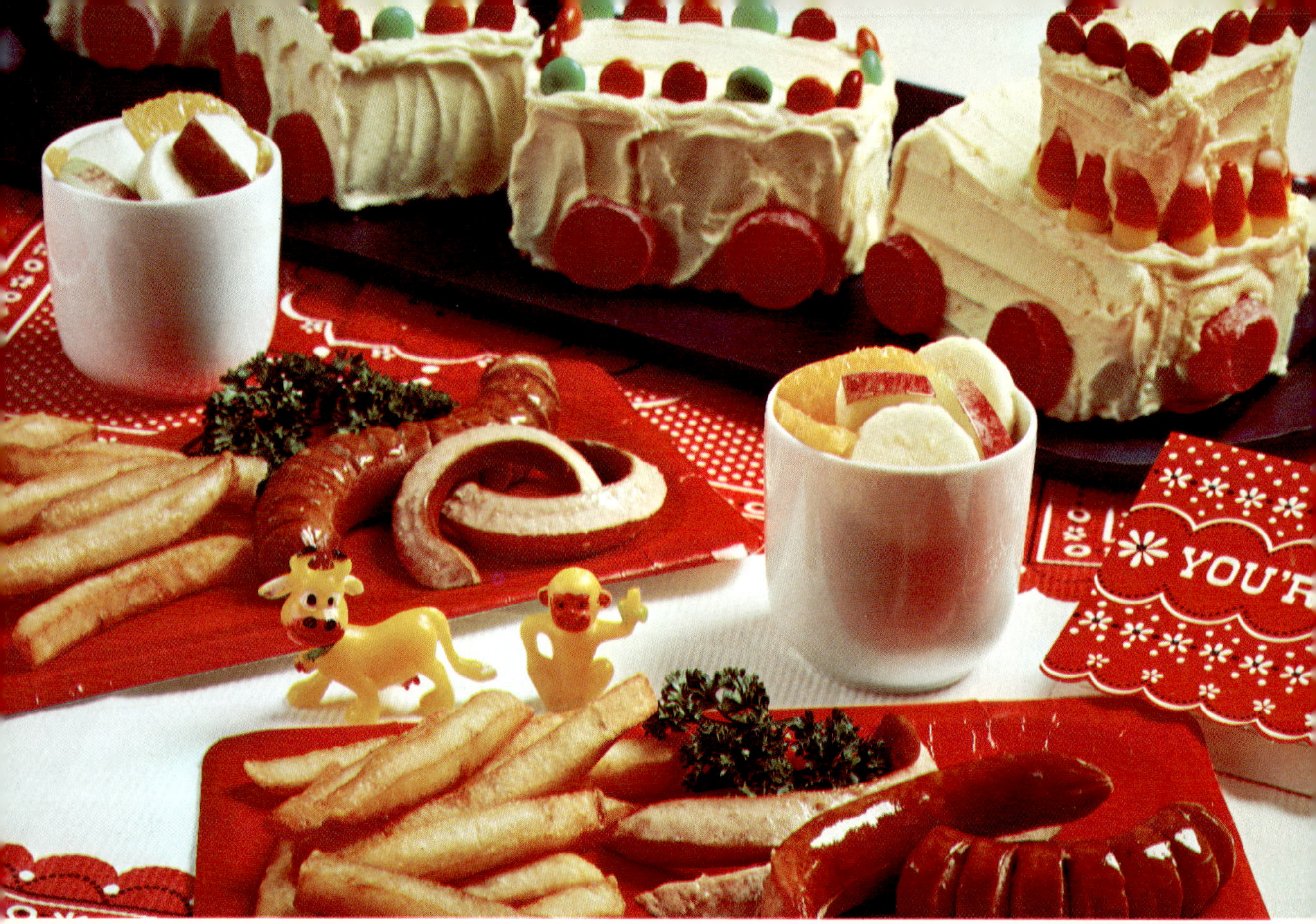
YOU'R

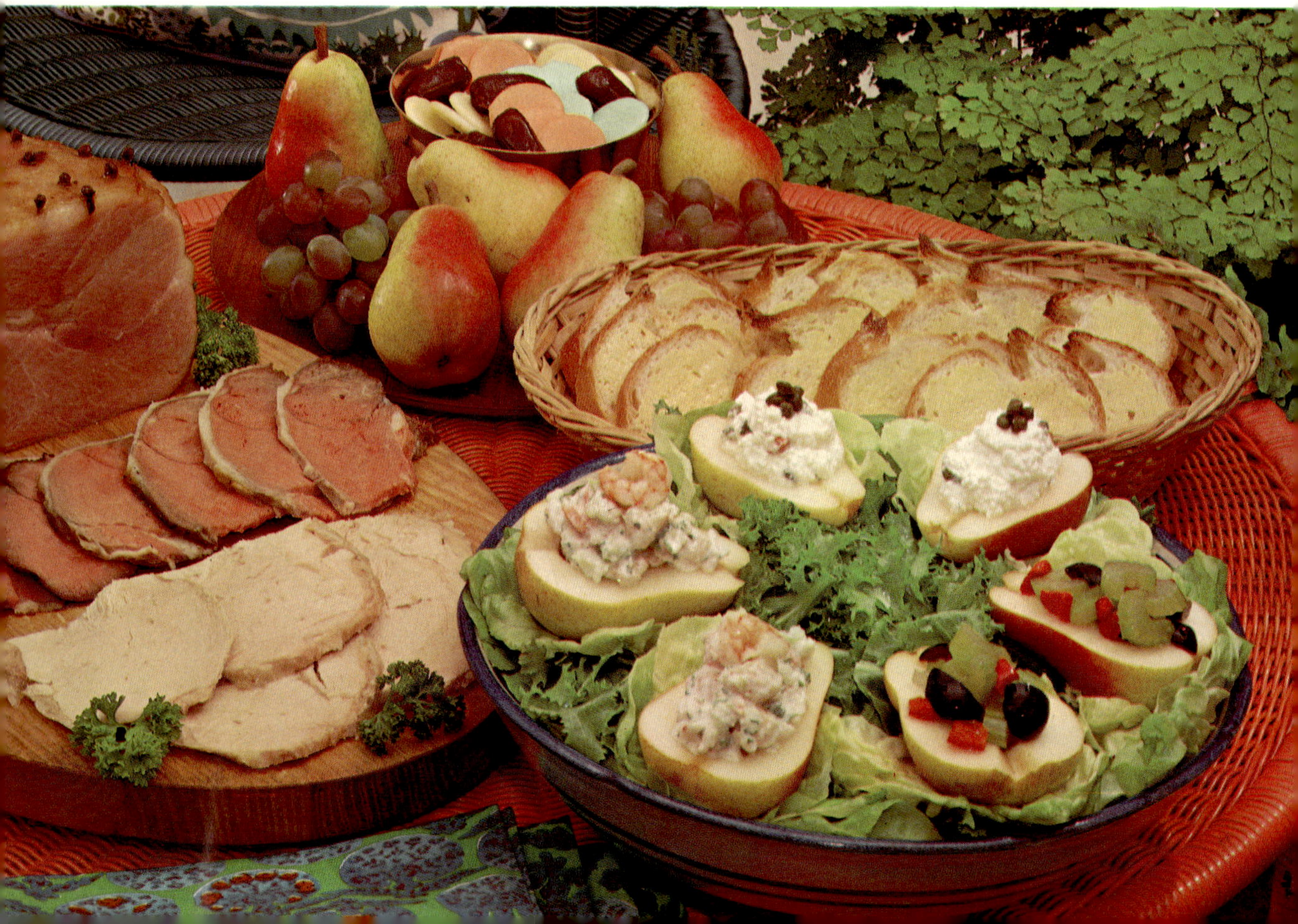

FEBRUARY Children's Parties

About half past February, winter can wear down youngsters, and Moms, too. When weather rules out beach or backyard play, fun will have to be of your own making.

If someone in the family has a February birthday, capitalize on it for a party that will keep the children busy for weeks making plans and preparations. With no built-in birthday, borrow one from Lincoln or Washington and have a patriotic party. Or choose a special interest theme, such as a Train Party for the boys.

If you're planning a girls' party, Valentine's Day offers a perfect opportunity for frills and femininity.

The factor that will decide most details of the party is the age of the child. Here are a few guidelines for preschool and schoolage groups.

PARTIES FOR PRESCHOOLERS

A longstanding rule of thumb for preschooler parties is to invite a number of guests equal to the child's age. While not an inflexible rule, it is good advice, since small children generally do better in small groups.

Give yourself plenty of time to plan a party that will keep the little ones busy. Decorations, games and party food all benefit from advance preparation.

PARTY THEME

Let your child's interests suggest the party theme, and carry it out in invitations, decorations, and games.

If he is, say, a train buff, cut red construction paper into caboose shapes for invitations that announce the time and place. Include your phone number and ask for a reply, so you know that the other mothers are aware of your plans. A week is plenty of notice for the under-five set.

First impressions are important to the success of parties for the pint-sized. For openers at your train party, you might attach a big railroad crossing sign or a travel poster to the front door.

GAMES

Once inside, the guest of honor or an older child could be stationed to issue each guest his "ticket." It could be half of a picture with the matching half hidden in some safe area of the house. Send him off to hunt for it while you await the rest of the guests. This gives him an excuse to explore his new surroundings. When the hidden half is found, have a small prize ready.

Prizes are a key element in the success of any party for children, so provide some sort of loot bag, labeled with the owner's name, to keep belongings straight. Gifts and prizes should be alike or similar in value. Lollipops, balloons,

TOP: Silly Dogs; Choo-Choo Cake
BOTTOM: Smorgasbord Pear Salads

FEBRUARY—CHILDREN'S PARTIES

pencils, puzzles, or homemade badges are inexpensive prizes children like. When passing out awards emphasize participation, not winning or losing.

Don't plan games that are too complex. It's better to stay with the familiar ones such as "pin the tail on the donkey" or "fishing pond." In that game, the guest drops a string from a pole over a stairway bannister while a helper hooks a prize to the end. But you can vary the games to match your party theme. For a train party, try "pinning the caboose on the train."

Plan plenty of games, about twice as many as you think you'll need, and round up all supplies for playing and prizes in advance. At party time, move quickly from one game to the next to keep things active.

TABLE DECORATIONS

It's possible to buy ready-made sets with coordinated tablecloth, centerpiece, plates, and napkins. But if you have the time, make your own decorations and enlist the youngsters' help.

Table favors could be trainmen's hats and red bandanas. Make the hats from striped pillow ticking gathered into a large circle for the crown and attach the crown to a headband and bill cut from stiff fabric.

Use your child's train set for centerpiece, or cut construction paper tracks to go around the table, with spurs out to each guest's place ending in nut cups. Or the centerpiece could be a choo-choo cake.

FOOD

Preschoolers generally have simple tastes. Grilled cheese, skinless franks, peanut butter and jelly, and egg salad are all child-approved sandwich fillings. Offer an assortment and the chance of pleasing everybody is greater.

Sandwich fillings may be plain, but the shapes can be as fancy as you want. Such whimsy will intrigue even the picky eaters. Accompany the sandwiches with such standbys as shoestring potatoes and fruit cups. The choo-choo cake will provide dessert. Make servings small. It's better to offer seconds than to throw any away. If you serve ice cream, have it dipped and waiting in the freezer, in muffin pans lined with paper baking cups. Scooping ice cream seems to take forever when you have an impatient crew waiting.

GRADE SCHOOLERS

Among the grade school set, tastes are much more defined. Your child will want to have a say about whom to invite and what to do at the party.

PARTY THEME

For children of a certain age, mixed parties are taboo. All-girl and all-boy parties are much preferred.

Suppose the party child is a girl, and she wants to invite five friends for lunch. Valentine's Day offers a ready-made theme, so make the most of it.

The invitations could be frilly valentines, or funny ones cut into jigsaw pieces. Or buy miniature heart-shaped candy boxes and tuck a note inside with all the party details; let the young hostess deliver these personally.

If you have the space, plan to separate the party game area from the dining room, so when it's time to serve, the table will come as a breathtaking surprise.

GAMES

As soon as the guests arrive, direct them to the game area and give them something to do. Inexpensive heart-shaped sewing cards can be precut and prepunched from cardboard. Thread some yarn through oversized needles and get the new arrivals involved at once. The finished sewing cards make nice take-home favors.

When all the guests have gathered and finished sewing, give each a bag marked with her name. Explain that candy hearts are hidden around the room, and start the hunt. Or hide a deck of playing cards and award a prize to the one finding the most hearts (and everyone else, too).

"Telephone" is a game favored by this age group. Seat the guests in a circle and have the first player whisper a short "telephone" message to the next, who whispers it to the next, and so on. The last girl in the circle repeats the message—or what she thinks she heard—aloud, followed by the original version. Give each player a chance to start the call.

Another favorite is the composite story. Ask the first girl to write the opening line of a thriller, and fold it under so it can't be seen by the second player, who adds a line, and so on. When the story makes the rounds, unfold the paper and have it read aloud.

TABLE DECORATIONS

Make the dining area a life-size valentine, lacy and picture-pretty. Run strips of red and white crepe paper from the ceiling light fixture to the tops of windows and doors. Attach a few balloons to the streamers, too, and suspend paper hearts from ribbons.

FEBRUARY—CHILDREN'S PARTIES

The centerpiece could be a heart-shaped cake, or a big valentine box like the ones at school with a gift inside for each guest.

Lacy plastic can be purchased by the yard for placemats or tablecloth. If there's time, use it to make a simple apron for each guest. Personalize the apron by writing the girl's name in bold letters across the front with colorful plastic tape. Hang one over each chair for a "place card."

FOOD
Like the menu for smaller children, keep food choices strictly in tune with your child's favorite foods. If it's lunchtime, offer a selection of sandwiches, vegetable strips and dunk, fruited gelatin, and milk. Party touches can be added, of course, as long as the foods are basically ones the children like. Sandwiches might be cut into heart or flower shapes, and the gelatin molded in heart shapes. A strawberry mix added to the milk adds a pretty note. Ice cream can also be pre-fashioned into fancy forms. And get out the pastry decorator and add the fanciest flourishes of all to the party cake.

TRAIN PARTY FOR PRESCHOOLERS

Silly Dogs

Shoestring Potatoes

Fruit Cup

Choo-Choo Cake

Ice Cream   Milk

Silly Dogs

1 pound (about 10) skinless franks
Water to cover
10 buns, hot dog and hamburger
Mustard, ketchup, pickle relish

1. Cut franks with a sharp knife to make the following shapes:

—Along one side, cut slits halfway into frank and ¼ inch apart up to middle. Turn frank over; repeat with opposite side from middle to end.

—Cut frankfurter in long quarters, making 4 separate strips.

—Make 3 parallel slits at each end of frankfurter, cutting toward center. Leave 1 inch in center of frank uncut.

—Cut frankfurter in half crosswise. Cut deep slits along one side of each half, ¼ inch apart.

2. Bring water to a boil. Pour over franks in a saucepan removed from heat. Cover and let stand 7 minutes. Franks will curl up into Silly Dog shapes.

3. Serve franks that have curled into a circle in hamburger buns; straight ones in hot dog buns. Serve with condiments.

About 10 servings

FEBRUARY—CHILDREN'S PARTIES

Choo-Choo Cake

1 package (2-layer size) yellow cake mix
1 package (2-layer size) vanilla frosting mix
Few drops yellow food coloring
Decorating trims: large gumdrops, candy corn, candy covered chocolate drops

1. Prepare cake according to package directions. Bake in a greased and floured 13×9-inch baking pan. Cool. Cut 4 pieces of cake 4×2½ inches each. Remove from pan. Cut a piece 2×1 inches for smoke stack.
2. Prepare frosting mix according to package directions, adding food coloring during mixing to give a pastel yellow color. Frost small pieces of cake on sides and top; frost smoke stack and place on 1 car of train to make engine.
3. Cut a slice off large end of gumdrops for wheels. Use short pieces of wooden picks to secure to sides of cake.
4. Decorate tops of each car with candy covered chocolate drops.
5. Decorate smoke stack with candy corn.
6. Press small end of a gumdrop into front of engine for light.
7. Place on tray to serve. Cut train cars in half to make 8 pieces. Frost remaining cake in pan with remaining frosting to serve to mothers in attendance.

GRADE SCHOOLERS' VALENTINE PARTY

Heartwarming Sandwiches
(Buffet of sandwiches cut in heart shapes, filled with cream and Cheddar cheese, peanut butter and jelly, and lunchmeat)

Tempting Tuna Dip

Carrot, Celery, and Green Pepper Strips

Party-Perfect Salad Molds

Sweetheart Cake

Ice Cream Slices decorated with Candy Hearts

Milk with Strawberry Flavoring Added

FEBRUARY—CHILDREN'S PARTIES

Tempting Tuna Dip

- 1 package (3 ounces) cream cheese, softened
- 1 cup dairy sour cream
- 1 can (7 ounces) tuna, drained and flaked
- 2 teaspoons chopped chives
- 1 teaspoon Worcestershire sauce
- ¼ teaspoon salt

1. Beat cream cheese and dairy sour cream together until fluffy.
2. Add tuna, chives, Worcestershire sauce, and salt; blend gently but thoroughly. Cover and let stand in refrigerator at least 2 hours to chill and blend flavors.

About 2 cups dip

Party-Perfect Salad Molds

- 2 packages (10 or 12 ounces each) frozen sliced peaches, thawed
- 2 packages (3 ounces each) strawberry-flavored gelatin
- 2 cups ginger ale
- ½ cup lemon juice
- ½ cup maraschino cherries, quartered
- ¼ cup chopped celery
- ¼ cup chopped green pepper

1. Drain and set peaches aside, reserving syrup. Add enough water to syrup to make 1½ cups; bring to boiling.
2. Add boiling liquid to gelatin in a bowl and stir until gelatin is dissolved. Mix in ginger ale and lemon juice.
3. Chill until slightly thicker than thick, unbeaten egg white.
4. Blend in peaches and remaining ingredients. Spoon into twelve ½-cup individual molds. Chill until firm.
5. Unmold onto chilled salad plates. Garnish as desired.

12 servings

Sweetheart Cake

- 3 cups sifted cake flour
- 1 tablespoon baking powder
- ½ teaspoon salt
- 1 cup butter or margarine
- 1 tablespoon vanilla extract
- 1 cup sugar
- 6 egg whites
- ¾ cup sugar
- 1 cup milk
- Pineapple Cream Filling
- Seven-Minute Frosting

1. Sift together flour, baking powder, and salt; set aside.
2. Cream butter and vanilla extract until butter is softened; add 1 cup sugar gradually, creaming until fluffy after each addition.
3. Beat egg whites until frothy; add ¾ cup sugar gradually, beating well after each addition; continue beating meringue until very stiff peaks are formed.
4. Alternately blend dry ingredients in fourths, milk in thirds into creamed mixture, beating only until smooth after each addition. (Do not overbeat.) Add the meringue to batter and fold in gently until well blended. Turn batter into two greased and waxed paper lined 9-inch round or heart-shape layer cake pans.
5. Bake at 350°F 30 to 35 minutes, or until cake tests done. Cool and remove from pans; peel off waxed paper.
6. Place 1 cake layer on cake plate and spread filling over top. Place other cake layer over filling. Frost sides and top of cake with frosting.
7. Using a **decorating gel** or **commercial tinted frosting** with decorating tip, write "Be my Valentine" on cake.

One 9-inch layer cake

Pineapple Cream Filling

1 cup milk
¼ cup sugar
1 tablespoon cornstarch
Few grains salt
1 egg, slightly beaten
1 can (8 ounces) crushed pineapple, drained
1 teaspoon vanilla extract

1. Scald ¾ cup milk.
2. Combine sugar, cornstarch, and salt in a saucepan. Add remaining milk, mixing well; gradually stir in scalded milk. Stirring gently and constantly, bring mixture to boiling; cook 3 minutes.
3. Vigorously stir about 3 tablespoons hot mixture into egg. Immediately blend into mixture in saucepan. Cook 3 to 5 minutes, stirring to keep mixture cooking evenly. Remove from heat. Cover and cool.
4. Stir in crushed pineapple and vanilla extract. Chill in refrigerator until ready to use.

About 1½ cups filling

Seven-Minute Frosting

1½ cups sugar
⅓ cup water
1 tablespoon light corn syrup
⅛ teaspoon salt
2 egg whites (unbeaten)
1 teaspoon vanilla extract

1. Combine sugar, water, corn syrup, salt, and egg whites in top of a double boiler; mix well.
2. Place over boiling water and immediately beat with rotary beater 7 to 10 minutes, or until mixture holds stiff peaks.
3. Remove from heat and add vanilla extract; beat until cool and thick enough to spread.

Enough to frost sides and tops of two 9-inch cake layers

Note: Mixture may be tinted by gently stirring in one or more drops food coloring.

OTHER CHOICES FOR CHILDREN'S PARTIES

Chocolate-Banana Frozen Pops

6 ripe bananas
1 package (6 ounces) semisweet chocolate pieces (1 cup)

1. Peel bananas and cut in halves crosswise. Insert a wooden stick into the end of each. Place in a shallow pan; freeze 2 to 3 hours.
2. Melt chocolate pieces over hot (not boiling) water.
3. Spread chocolate with spatula over each banana. Chocolate will become firm immediately.
4. Wrap each banana in aluminum foil and store in freezer.

12 frozen pops

Double-Quick Cookie Squares

2½ cups graham cracker crumbs
1 package (6 ounces) semisweet chocolate pieces
½ cup flaked coconut
1 can (14 ounces) sweetened condensed milk
½ cup chopped pecans

1. Put graham cracker crumbs into a bowl. Add chocolate pieces, coconut, and sweetened condensed milk; blend to moisten cracker crumbs. Turn into a lightly greased 9-inch square pan. Top with nuts.
2. Bake at 325°F 30 minutes. (Cookies are moist and brown only slightly.) Cool in pan on wire rack. Cut into squares.

3 dozen cookies

MARCH
Progressive Dinner Party

Hostesses of the world, unite! Organize your own Progressive Dinner Party and enjoy shorter working hours plus fringe benefits. These include being able to entertain more often, because the work, the expense, and the fun are shared.

Those who have already jumped on the bandwagon claim that the Progressive Party is the best solution for the overworked hostess. It's more fun for guests, too, as it lets them sample the hospitality of several homes rather than just one.

Here's how a progressive dinner works. The first course, usually punch and appetizers, is served at one home. After a hospitality hour, the group moves on to the next house for the main course. Salad or dessert is served at a third home, and if another stop is desired, it can be for fruit and cheese with cordials.

Today few people have help aside from those mechanical ones that whip, blend, cook, and store our food. But through cooperative efforts, the progressive dinner party does provide help of the best sort.

HOW TO ORGANIZE A PROGRESSIVE DINNER PARTY

Since the party will be a joint effort, plans will have to be coordinated. If you are the organizer, call a few friends at least a month before the party date. Arrangements can be made by phone, but it's even better to have a pre-party party—a coffee break, perhaps—to talk it over.

The guest list will be a first consideration. Decide whether to limit it to the host couples, or to expand the party with each host inviting one or two other couples and paying the cost of his guests. It's a good idea to divide costs evenly among the hosts.

Next order of business is menu. Details should be coordinated to avoid duplication or conflict in flavors. Try to select dishes that are do-ahead, so that no one need worry about last minute cooking. Strive to make each course equal in interest. A progressive dinner shouldn't become a contest among hostesses—that would spoil the fun.

Decide whether this is a party for games and activities, or whether the progression of the party itself will provide all the activity needed. If the group isn't well acquainted, a mixer game during the hospitality hour might be a good idea. Or if you reach the final house earlier than expected, you might like to be prepared to dance or play parlor games.

Here are a few suggestions for each stage of your progressive dinner party:

THE HOSPITALITY HOUR

Offering a punch, alcoholic or nonalcoholic, with appetizers, is a good way to begin a progressive

24   MARCH—PROGRESSIVE DINNER PARTY

dinner party. It's more considerate to set out two punch bowls, one "with" and one "without," than to let the teetotallers settle for a bottle of pop.

Even the spiked punch bowl can be rather mild if you are planning to serve wine with the following courses. A bottle of champagne or other wine mixed in equal parts with sparkling water plus a touch of cointreau, crème de menthe, or some other variant, delivers the right degree of "punch"—not a double whammy. There's more to come!

THE MAIN COURSE

Since this course generally involves more dishes than the others, a co-hostess could be assigned. Meat and pasta or potatoes are elements of the usual main course. If the hostess is preparing a roast, it could go in the oven just as she leaves for the hospitality hour, timed to come out as she returns. A meat casserole, such as lasagne, could be prepared and frozen weeks ahead of the party.

To allow ample defrosting time, transfer it to the refrigerator a day ahead of the party. The microwave oven works miracles at serving time, converting food from frosty to toasty in minutes. Remember to freeze in a glass casserole or other microwave-safe container.

The main course seems more festive with a wine accompaniment. Follow the old rule: red wine with red meat and white wine with white, such as fish or chicken. If red is the choice, open the bottle and, if necessary, decant before leaving for the hospitality hour. Red wine benefits from the chance to "breathe."

THE SALAD COURSE

If the salad is a separate course, serve it with flair. Remember your visits to restaurants where the salad was prepared at the table? Borrow some of that drama for your own salad creation. Bring all the ingredients to the dining room, mix the dressing and toss the greens at the table. Or perhaps you'd like to borrow another restaurant idea. Set up a salad bar with all the fixings, and let the guests serve themselves. Wine is optional; vinegary dressings conflict with the flavor of the wine.

THE DESSERT COURSE

Like the salad course, this course stands on its own, so it must be something fairly striking. As with the salad, a dramatic presentation will be well worth the effort. Cherry Flambée and Bananas Foster Brennan's lend themselves to tableside preparation yet neither is an overly heavy conclusion to a meal. Chocolate Fondue lets everyone in on the act. If you prefer to have everything done in advance, try Peppermint Stick Charlotte.

FRUIT AND CHEESE COURSE

If this last course is included, it won't require showmanship; just a few perfect specimens of the fruits and cheeses you select. Brandy, liqueur, or a dessert wine make harmonious partners for this final course.

APPETIZERS

Gala Pecan Spread

- 1 package (8 ounces) cream cheese, softened
- 2 tablespoons milk
- 1 jar (2½ ounces) sliced dried beef, finely cut with scissors
- ¼ cup finely chopped green pepper
- 2 tablespoons dried onion flakes
- ½ teaspoon garlic salt
- ¼ teaspoon pepper
- ½ cup dairy sour cream
- ½ cup coarsely chopped pecans
- 2 tablespoons butter or margarine
- ¼ teaspoon salt

1. Combine cheese and milk; mix well.
2. Stir in dried beef, green pepper, and dry seasonings. Mix in sour cream. Spoon into a small ovenproof bowl.
3. Combine pecans, butter, and salt in a small skillet. Heat until pecans are lightly browned, stirring occasionally.
4. Sprinkle nuts over cheese mixture.
5. Bake at 250°F 20 minutes.
6. Serve hot with **crackers**.

About 2 cups spread

Swedish Lemon Meatballs

- 1 pound ground beef
- 1½ pounds ground pork
- 1 cup cracker crumbs
- 2 eggs, slightly beaten
- 1 package dry onion soup mix, divided
- 2 teaspoons salt
- ¼ teaspoon nutmeg
- ¼ teaspoon allspice
- ¼ teaspoon pepper
- Grated peel of 1 lemon
- Cooking oil

Gravy:
- ¼ cup all-purpose flour
- 2½ cups water
- 1 tablespoon lemon juice

1. Combine meat, cracker crumbs, eggs, ¼ cup of the onion soup mix, salt, nutmeg, allspice, pepper, and lemon peel. Handle no more than necessary to mix ingredients.
2. Using measuring teaspoon, dip out portion for each ball and roll into shape. Brown in cooking oil. Brown only as many meatballs at one time as will fit easily into frying pan.
3. After browning a batch, transfer to a large baking pan or roaster. When all are browned, add ¼ cup cooking oil to frying pan.
4. For gravy, sprinkle flour over fat. When it bubbles up, pour in water gradually, stirring constantly.
5. Add remainder of onion soup mix and let simmer for a few minutes. Add lemon juice and pour over meatballs.
6. Cover and bake in a 350°F oven for 35 to 40 minutes.

About 125 meatballs

Note: These can be made ahead and refrigerated or frozen until the day of the party. Heat and serve.

Appetizer Party Pie

- 1 round loaf rye bread (unsliced)
- 2 packages (3 ounces each) cream cheese, softened
- ¼ cup mayonnaise
- 1 jar (2 ounces) lumpfish caviar
- 3 hard-cooked eggs
- 1 cucumber, scored along sides with fork and sliced
- Cherry tomatoes, sliced
- Pimento-stuffed olives, sliced

1. Trim bottom crust off round loaf. Cut into four slices crosswise to form large rounds of bread. To make cuts, first go around loaf with a shallow cut to make slice about ⅜ inch thick. Then, rotating loaf on its side, make deeper cut to go all the way through.
2. Beat softened cream cheese and mayonnaise together. Divide between 4 slices and spread evenly to edge of each slice.
3. Make a circle in center of each slice with caviar.
4. Force yolk of one egg through sieve. Spoon ring of sieved yolk around each caviar center.
5. Make next ring of one of the following: sliced hard-cooked egg, sliced pimento-stuffed olives, or cucumber rings. If space is left at rim, complete with contrasting garnish. Double layers can also be formed, such as tomato slices atop cucumbers.
6. Use any remaining caviar for accents between other trim.
7. Cover with plastic wrap and store in refrigerator. At serving time, cut into wedges and serve.

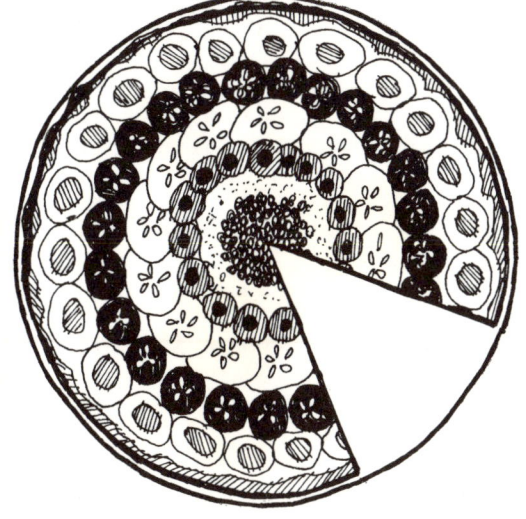

GREEK DINNER

Greek Salad

- 2 quarts mixed greens, such as iceberg lettuce, Bibb lettuce, romaine, escarole, chicory
- 2 medium tomatoes, cut in wedges
- 1 medium cucumber, thinly sliced
- 1 small onion, thinly sliced
- ½ green pepper, chopped
- ½ cup ripe olives
- ½ cup feta cheese, crumbled
- ½ cup olive oil
- 3 tablespoons lemon juice or wine vinegar
- 1 teaspoon oregano
- ½ teaspoon salt
- Dash pepper
- 1 can (2 ounces) anchovy fillets, drained

1. Toss greens with vegetables, olives, and feta cheese, reserving 2 tablespoons cheese for garnish.
2. For dressing, mix oil, lemon juice, oregano, salt, and pepper in a jar and shake well.
3. Toss salad and dressing. Sprinkle with reserved cheese and top with anchovy fillets.

6 servings

Pastitsio (Greek Pasta Casserole)

- 1 medium onion, chopped
- 2 tablespoons cooking oil
- 1 pound ground beef
- 1 teaspoon salt
- ¼ teaspoon thyme
- 1 can (16 ounces) tomatoes
- 1 can (6 ounces) tomato paste
- 1 package (8 ounces) elbow macaroni
- 1 tablespoon butter
- 4 egg whites (unbeaten)
- ½ cup crumbled feta cheese (may be omitted if unavailable)
- ½ cup butter or margarine
- ½ cup all-purpose flour
- 1 teaspoon salt

1. Sauté onion in cooking oil until tender. Add beef and cook until it is no longer pink. Add salt, thyme, tomatoes, and tomato paste and simmer, uncovered, 30 minutes, stirring occasionally.
2. Meanwhile, cook macaroni according to package directions.
3. When beef mixture has completed simmering, remove from heat to cool slightly.
4. Drain the macaroni; add 1 tablespoon butter. Mix in egg whites and feta cheese.
5. Combine macaroni mixture with meat mixture. Pour into a greased 13×9×2-inch baking pan.
6. Melt ½ cup butter in a saucepan over low heat. Blend in flour, salt, and ¼ teaspoon cinnamon. Heat until bubbly. Add milk slowly, stirring constantly. When the mixture bubbles and has thickened, remove from heat. Cool slightly.

¼ teaspoon cinnamon
1 quart milk
4 egg yolks, slightly beaten
Cinnamon

7. Stir a small amount of the sauce into the egg yolks. Add this mixture to the sauce, stirring rapidly. When the sauce is smooth, pour over the meat combination in the baking pan. Sprinkle lightly with cinnamon.
8. Bake at 375°F 30 minutes, or until the topping is set and is firm when tested with a knife.

12 servings

Note: This casserole may be assembled early and refrigerated. Allow 15 minutes longer in the oven.

CONTINENTAL CUISINE

Asparagus Vinaigrette

1 envelope herb-flavored oil-and-vinegar salad dressing mix
Tarragon-flavored white wine vinegar
Water
Salad oil
2 tablespoons chopped parsley
1 tablespoon finely chopped chives
2 teaspoons capers
1 hard-cooked egg, finely chopped
Cooked asparagus spears, chilled

1. Prepare salad dressing mix as directed on package, using vinegar, water, and salad oil.
2. Using 1 cup of the dressing, mix well with parsley, chives, capers, and egg. Chill thoroughly.
3. To serve, arrange chilled asparagus in 6 bundles on a chilled serving plate lined with **Boston lettuce**. Garnish each bundle with a **pimento strip**. Complete platter with **cucumber slices** and **radish roses**. Mix dressing well before spooning over asparagus.

6 servings

Veal Epicurean

1 tablespoon olive oil
1 tablespoon butter or margarine
2 pounds veal cutlets, cut in 2×½-inch strips
2 tablespoons flour
¾ teaspoon salt
⅛ teaspoon pepper
1 cup chicken broth
1 cup dry white wine
1 pound small white onions, peeled
12 sprigs parsley, chopped
1 bay leaf
½ pound small fresh mushrooms
3 tablespoons butter or margarine

1. Heat olive oil and butter in a heavy skillet. Add meat and brown on all sides. Remove from skillet to a 1¼-quart casserole having a cover; set aside.
2. Stir a mixture of flour, salt, and pepper into drippings in skillet. Add the broth gradually, blending thoroughly. Bring rapidly to boiling, stirring constantly; cook 1 to 2 minutes; remove from heat.
3. Blend in wine, onions, and parsley. Pour over veal in casserole; add bay leaf.
4. Cover and bake at 325°F about 1 hour, or until meat is tender.
5. Cook mushrooms in the 3 tablespoons butter about 5 minutes. Add to casserole and bake about 15 minutes longer.

6 to 8 servings

Creamy Green Noodles

- 3 tablespoons flour
- 1 teaspoon salt
- Few grains pepper
- 2 tablespoons butter or margarine
- 2 cups cream
- ¼ cup sliced pimento-stuffed olives
- 8 ounces green noodles, cooked and drained
- ¼ cup shredded Parmesan cheese
- 2 teaspoons grated lemon peel

1. Blend a mixture of flour, salt, and pepper into hot butter in a saucepan. Heat until bubbly. Remove from heat. Add cream gradually, stirring constantly. Bring to boiling and cook 1 to 2 minutes.
2. Toss olives and sauce with noodles; turn into a warm serving dish. Sprinkle a mixture of Parmesan cheese and lemon peel evenly over top.

About 6 servings

FRENCH DINNER

Roast Leg of Lamb, French Style

- 5- to 6-pound lamb leg (do not remove fell)
- 2 teaspoons salt
- ¼ teaspoon pepper
- Garlic cloves, cut in slivers
- Melted butter or margarine

1. Rub lamb with a mixture of the salt and pepper. Cut several small slits in surface of meat and insert a sliver of garlic in each.
2. Place lamb, skin side down, on rack in a roasting pan. Insert meat thermometer so tip is slightly beyond center of thickest part of meat; be sure that it does not rest in fat or on bone.
3. Roast, uncovered, at 325°F 2 to 3 hours, allowing 25 to 30 minutes per pound. Brush meat frequently with melted butter during roasting. Meat is medium done when thermometer registers 160°F and is well done at 170–180°F.
4. Remove meat to a warm serving platter and garnish with mint or parsley sprigs, if desired.

About 10 servings

Rice Soubise

- ¼ cup butter
- 2 pounds onions, peeled and thinly sliced
- ½ cup uncooked regular rice
- 1 teaspoon salt
- ⅛ teaspoon pepper
- ¼ cup whipping cream
- ¼ cup shredded Swiss cheese
- 2 tablespoons butter
- 1 tablespoon minced parsley

1. Melt butter in a shallow casserole. Stir in onion, rice, salt, and pepper. Cover tightly.
2. Cook in a 300°F oven 1¼ to 1½ hours, or until rice and onion are very tender.
3. Just before serving, stir in cream, cheese, and remaining 2 tablespoons butter. Sprinkle with parsley.

About 8 servings

Salade Provençale

2 green peppers, cut in strips
¼ cup oil (part salad oil and part olive oil)
3 firm ripe tomatoes, washed and cut in pieces
½ Bermuda onion, peeled and sliced
4 ounces fresh mushrooms, cleaned and sliced lengthwise
12 whole pitted ripe olives

1. Fry the green pepper strips in the oil until partially tender.
2. Remove strips to a bowl. Add the tomatoes, onion, mushrooms, and olives; toss.
3. Shake well in a covered jar, 4 parts **oil** (half salad oil and half olive oil, including the oil from frying), 1 part **white wine vinegar**, **salt** and **pepper** to taste, and **1 cut clove garlic**. Remove garlic and pour dressing over salad; toss gently until well coated. Marinate at room temperature about 1 hour, turning occasionally. Chill.
4. Sprinkle generously with **freshly ground black pepper**.

About 6 servings

DESSERTS

Peppermint Stick Charlotte

2 envelopes unflavored gelatin
¾ cup sugar, divided
¼ teaspoon salt
4 eggs, separated
2½ cups milk
8 drops red food coloring
⅔ cup finely crushed peppermint stick candy
10 ladyfingers
1 cup whipping cream, whipped

1. In medium saucepan mix gelatin, ¼ cup sugar, and salt.
2. Beat together egg yolks and milk; stir into gelatin mixture. Place over low heat; stir constantly until gelatin dissolves and mixture thickens slightly, about 5 minutes. Remove from heat and cool slightly.
3. Stir in red food coloring and crushed peppermint candy. Chill, stirring occasionally, until mixture mounds slightly when dropped from a spoon.
4. Meanwhile, separate ladyfingers and stand around side of 9-inch springform pan, rounded side against the pan.
5. Beat egg whites until soft peaks form. Gradually beat in remaining ½ cup sugar and beat until stiff peaks form. Fold into chilled gelatin mixture. Fold in whipped cream and turn into prepared pan. Chill until set.
6. To serve, remove sides of pan and garnish with additional whipped cream and crushed peppermint candy.

8 to 10 servings

Chocolate Fondue

- 4 packages (6 ounces each) milk chocolate pieces or semisweet chocolate pieces
- 2 cups (1 pint) light corn syrup
- 1 tablespoon vanilla extract
- ½ cup cream, brandy, or rum
- Assorted dippers (marshmallows, strawberries with hulls, apple slices, banana chunks, pineapple chunks, mandarin orange segments, cherries with stems, cake cubes, melon balls)

1. Combine chocolate pieces and corn syrup in a heavy saucepan. Heat and stir until chocolate melts and mixture is smooth.
2. Add vanilla extract (omit if using brandy or rum) and cream; stir until well blended. Turn into a fondue pot and keep hot.
3. To serve, surround fondue pot with small bowls of dippers. Provide fondue forks for guests to spear dippers, then dip into fondue.

About 4 cups

Bananas Foster Brennan's

- 1 tablespoon butter
- 2 teaspoons brown sugar
- Dash ground cinnamon
- 1 firm ripe banana, cut crosswise in 4 pieces
- 2 tablespoons warm rum
- 1 teaspoon warm banana liqueur

1. Heat butter, brown sugar, and cinnamon in a chafing dish; add banana and sauté until tender.
2. Pour rum and banana liqueur over banana and flame the spirit.

1 serving

Cherry Flambée

- 1 pound fresh or thawed frozen Bing cherries
- ¼ cup firmly packed brown sugar
- 2 tablespoons butter
- ¼ cup Cointreau
- ¼ cup kirsch
- 1 tablespoon lemon juice

1. Rinse and drain fresh cherries; remove and discard the cherry stems and pits.
2. Put into skillet over medium heat brown sugar and butter. Stir until butter is melted and sugar is dissolved.
3. Mix in Cointreau, kirsch, lemon juice, and cherries. Stir gently until liqueurs are thoroughly heated.
4. Ignite with match until flames appear. Serve immediately with **ice cream.**

About 8 servings

APRIL
Bachelor's Brunch

Brunch and the bachelor have been keeping company for years. Small wonder, when this little meal lets him chalk up maximum points for hostmanship with a minimum of effort.

Early spring is a busy brunch season for the bachelor, since it gives him a chance to make good the social obligations he's been collecting all winter. His kitchen, perhaps his whole apartment, may be small, but he'll get the most from what he has at brunch. With a shrewd selection of recipes that look more difficult than they really are, he can win laurels—and perhaps a few new invitations!

There are no hard and fast rules about brunch, other than it be a relatively early-day meal to serve the purpose of both breakfast and lunch. Purists may argue, but a bachelor brunch may start as easily after noon as before.

Beyond that, here are a few flexible guidelines.

INVITATIONS

Written invitations are fine, but unless he has a willing secretary, the bachelor would rather phone. Guests like a week's notice; more if the spring calendar is full of parties. The guest list shouldn't exceed seating space. Standing is all right at a cocktail party, but hard to manage at brunch. Table service isn't necessary; trays work fine as long as there's a place to sit comfortably.

THE MENU

Serve a cocktail that's a bit of a conversation piece. Our Spring Tonic, for example, is right in season and will have guests asking "What's in it?" Pair the alcoholic cocktails with a choice for the non-drinker, such as orange juice, which looks just like the Spring Tonic.

A bit of visiting over that eye-opener will prepare guests for the main dish, preferably one made hours or even days ahead of the party. A tuna or meat pie is a good choice because it combines protein, pastry, and vegetable in one delectable concoction. Have it all assembled, and as the first guest arrives, pop it in the oven. By the time you're ready for it, it will be ready for you.

Team the meat or tuna pie with a Spinach Mushroom Salad for chilly contrast in color and texture.

Or if suave sophistication is your game, Chicken Livers in Wild Rice Ring is your dish. Well before the party, simmer the chicken livers in a heavenly wine sauce. While cocktails are served, cook the rice, pack it into a ring mold, turn it out on a platter, and serve with the chicken livers. Reputations are built on such fare!

Crepes are another stellar brunch choice. They can be made at your convenience, a day or so in advance, when any failures will go unobserved. At serving time, only your successes are counted!

APRIL—BACHELOR'S BRUNCH

Early on the day of your brunch, place the pre-made crepes in muffin pans. Fill them with flaked salmon and a rich cheese custard. When the doorbell rings, start them baking while you enjoy a drink with your guests. At serving time, bring out the Salmon Quiche Crepes with a tart avocado and grapefruit salad.

Dessert isn't essential at brunchtime. A fruit bowl centerpiece can double as dessert, or you can pass a plate of candy. Or skip dessert altogether.

GERRY'S BRUNCH

Choice of Silver Gin Fizz or Orange Juice

Topsy Turvy Tuna Pie

Black-Eyed Devils

Spinach Mushroom Salad

Fresh Fruit Bowl

Silver Gin Fizz

- 8 ounces gin
- 2 ounces orange juice
- 4 lemons, juiced
- 2 tablespoons confectioners' sugar
  Cracked ice (6 or more cups)
- 2 egg whites
- 4 ounces cream

1. In an electric blender, combine gin, orange juice, lemon juice, confectioners' sugar, and 2 cups cracked ice; blend well.
2. Pour half the mixture into a container to reserve for second batch.
3. To remaining contents of the blender, add 1 more cup cracked ice, 1 egg white, and 2 ounces cream; blend again. Add ice until mixture reaches the consistency of a milk shake. Serve in chilled stemmed glasses.
4. Repeat step 3 with remaining mixture.

8 to 12 servings (depending upon capacity of glasses)

Nectarine Ripple Ice Cream;
Nectarine-Pineapple Sundae Sauce;
Nectarine Chiffon Cake

APRIL—BACHELOR'S BRUNCH

Topsy-Turvy Tuna Pie

- 1 lemon
- 1 green pepper
- 1 can (7 ounces) water-pack tuna, drained
- 1 small onion, finely chopped
- ¼ cup bread crumbs
- ½ teaspoon dry mustard
- 1 tablespoon lemon juice
- ½ cup ketchup
- 1 egg, well beaten
- ¼ pound sharp Cheddar cheese, sliced
- 1 cup all-purpose biscuit mix
- ½ cup milk

1. Cut unpeeled lemon into thin slices, remove seeds, and arrange over bottom of a well-greased 8-inch round layer cake pan.
2. Cut 1 ring from green pepper and put in center of cake pan. Finely chop remaining green pepper.
3. In a mixing bowl combine tuna, green pepper, onion, bread crumbs, dry mustard, lemon juice, ketchup, and egg. Spread mixture over lemon and green pepper in pan. Cover with a layer of cheese.
4. Mix biscuit mix and milk to a soft dough. Spread dough over cheese.
5. Bake at 400°F 20 to 30 minutes, or until biscuit topping is lightly browned.
6. Turn out onto a serving platter with biscuit layer on bottom and lemon slices on top.

6 to 8 servings

Black-Eyed Devils

- 1 dozen large eggs
- Dairy sour half-and-half (½ to ¾ cup)
- 2 tablespoons instant minced onion
- 2 teaspoons dry mustard
- 1 teaspoon salt
- 8 drops Tabasco
- 9 small ripe olives, finely chopped

1. Put cold eggs into a dish of lukewarm water to prevent cracked shells. Bring water in a large saucepan to rapid boiling, using enough water to come 1 inch above eggs. Transfer eggs from warm water to boiling water with a spoon; reduce heat to keep water below simmering and cook 20 minutes. Cool eggs promptly and thoroughly in cold water. Remove shells.
2. Carefully cut eggs in half; put yolks into a sieve over a bowl and reserve whites. Force yolks through sieve. Blend in half of the sour half-and-half. Add onion, dry mustard, salt, and Tabasco; mix well. Blend in desired amount of remaining sour half-and-half.
3. Stuff the egg-white halves with the yolk mixture. Sprinkle olives on top. Refrigerate several hours or overnight before serving.

24 stuffed egg halves

Spinach Mushroom Salad

- 1 bag (10 ounces) fresh spinach
- 6 slices bacon
- 1 box (5 ounces) fresh mushrooms
- 1 bunch green onions (6 to 8)
- ½ cup salad oil
- 2 tablespoons lemon juice or wine vinegar
- 1 clove garlic, minced
- 1 teaspoon salt
- ½ teaspoon dry mustard
- ¼ teaspoon sugar
- ¼ teaspoon pepper
- 1 egg yolk

1. Wash spinach and pat dry on absorbent paper; discard stems. Chill until serving time.
2. Fry bacon until crisp and remove to absorbent paper to drain; crumble.
3. Clean mushrooms; slice lengthwise through caps and stems.
4. Clean green onions; chop onions using some of the green tops for color.
5. For dressing, put remaining ingredients into an electric blender and run on medium speed until well blended.
6. At serving time, combine spinach, mushrooms, onion, and bacon in a salad bowl. Add dressing and toss.

6 servings

Onion Confetti Relish;
Savory Onion Topper;
Marinated Onion-Topped Burger Loaf;
Crispy French Fried Onion Rings

APRIL—BACHELOR'S BRUNCH

SPRING TONIC BRUNCH

Choice of Spring Tonic or Orange Juice

Chicken Livers in Wild Rice Ring

Fruit Cup

Toasted English Muffins   Jelly

Spring Tonic

1½ cups orange juice
1 cup gin
½ cup apricot brandy

1. Combine ingredients; stir.
2. Store in refrigerator until serving time. Serve in on-the-rocks glasses over **ice cubes**.

6 (4-ounce) servings

Chicken Livers in Wild Rice Ring

½ cup butter
1 pound chicken livers
1 bunch (6 to 8) green onions, chopped
1 box (5 ounces) fresh mushrooms, cleaned and sliced
1 cup chopped parsley
½ cup white wine
½ cup chicken broth
1 package (6 or 6¾ ounces) seasoned wild and white rice mix
Dairy sour cream (optional)

1. In a large skillet with cover, melt butter. Add livers, onions, mushrooms, and parsley. Sauté until livers show no trace of pink and onions are translucent.
2. Add wine and broth, cover, and simmer 10 minutes.
3. Prepare seasoned rice mix according to package directions.
4. Butter a 1-quart ring mold. When rice is done, turn into mold, packing down gently with spoon. Invert onto a warm serving platter and lift off mold.
5. Spoon hot chicken liver mixture into center of rice ring just before serving. Top with a dollop of sour cream, if desired.

About 6 servings

BRUNCH, BACHELOR STYLE

Choice of Bloody Mary Cocktails or Tomato Juice

Salmon Quiche Crepes

Avocado and Grapefruit Segments on Bibb Lettuce with Celery Seed Salad Dressing

Purchased Bon Bons

Bloody Mary

- 3 jiggers tomato juice
- 1½ jiggers vodka
- 2 to 3 teaspoons lemon juice
- ½ teaspoon Worcestershire sauce
- Pinch salt
- Dash Angostura bitters
- 2 ice cubes

Put ingredients into an electric blender. Blend 10 seconds; strain into a highball glass.

1 serving

Salmon Quiche Crepes

- 1 can (7¾ ounces) salmon
- 12 crepes (see below)
- ¾ cup shredded Swiss cheese
- ¼ cup grated Parmesan cheese
- 1 teaspoon fresh or freeze dried chives
- 2 eggs, beaten
- 1 cup half-and-half
- ¼ teaspoon salt
- ¼ teaspoon Worcestershire sauce
- Dash white pepper

1. Drain and flake salmon, removing bones and skin.
2. Carefully fit crepes, browner side down, in 12 greased muffin-pan wells.
3. Mix salmon, cheeses, and chives; spoon into crepe-lined muffin pans.
4. Combine beaten eggs, half-and-half, and seasonings. Pour over salmon and cheese.
5. Bake at 350°F 35 to 40 minutes, or until filling is set.

12 filled crepes

Crepes: In an electric blender container, combine **1½ cups milk, 1⅓ cups all-purpose flour, 3 eggs, 2 tablespoons oil or cooled melted butter, 1 teaspoon sugar, and ¼ teaspoon salt**; blend 30 seconds. Push unblended flour down with rubber spatula and blend 1 minute longer. Repeat if needed. Or beat with rotary beater until smooth. Let batter stand at room temperature 1 hour. Heat a little **butter** in a 5- to 7-inch crepe pan or heavy skillet. For each crepe add about 2 tablespoons batter, tilting pan to distribute evenly. Cook, turning once, until lightly browned on both sides. Crepes may be made ahead and refrigerated or frozen until needed.

APRIL—BACHELOR'S BRUNCH

Avocado and Grapefruit Segments on Bibb Lettuce

  2 large pink grapefruit
  2 ripe avocados
 12 crisp Bibb lettuce leaves (cup shape)

1. With a sharp knife, cut away peel and white membrane from grapefruit. Remove sections by cutting on either side of the dividing membranes; remove, section by section, over a bowl to collect juice. Discard seeds, if any. Store sections in refrigerator until time to assemble salads.
2. Peel avocados and cut into lengthwise slices. Toss in reserved grapefruit juice; store in juice in refrigerator until time to assemble salads.
3. For each serving, arrange 2 Bibb lettuce leaves on a plate and top with alternate slices of avocado and sections of grapefruit.
4. Serve with Celery Seed Salad Dressing.

6 servings

Celery Seed Salad Dressing

  ¼ cup sugar
  ⅓ cup light corn syrup
  ¼ cup vinegar
 1½ to 2 teaspoons celery seed
  1 teaspoon dry mustard
  1 teaspoon salt
    Few grains white pepper
  1 teaspoon grated onion
  1 cup salad oil

1. Combine all ingredients except the oil in a small bowl. Beat with a hand rotary beater until mixture is thoroughly blended.
2. Add the oil very gradually beating constantly. Continue beating until mixture thickens.
3. Chill thoroughly in covered container in refrigerator. Shake well before serving.

About 2 cups

May Bridal Showers

May flowers are supposed to follow April showers, but as it happens, May has quite a few showers of its own. That's because May, with temperatures warming and gardens unfolding, is the perfect time for a party with a romantic theme.

GUEST LIST

Unless the shower is meant to come as a surprise, ask the guest of honor for names of people she'd like you to invite. Then sound her out on preferred gifts. Gifts should never upstage sociability in your plans, but a few suggestions will help your guests to shop.

INVITATIONS

Spread the word about the party, by mail or phone, at least two weeks before the date. This will allow shopping time and insure a good turnout. Buy or make invitations to suit your party theme. If the shower is to be a surprise, mention it in the invitation.

MENU

Whether you serve a meal or only dessert depends upon the time of day. For an afternoon or after-dinner party, a punch and appetizers are just right. Conclude with a fancy dessert.

For a midday meal, consider a salad luncheon. This alternative is not only picture pretty, it's light in calories, too. Take your choice of a salad buffet or a salad bar.

THE SALAD BUFFET

An assortment of prepared-ahead salads offers a banquet of choice; the more the merrier. Hot, cold, fish, and fowl—variety is the key to success. There are two ways to produce a salad buffet.

The Hostess Does the Mostess: Everything for this menu is hostess-done. That means getting a really early start on preparations and stashing as many items as possible into the freezer and refrigerator prior to the party.

Salad Potluck: A few of the guests are asked to bring a salad and others contribute dessert or rolls. This carries the double advantage of reducing the hostess's work and increasing the variety. Arrange the party as a Gourmet Shower for the bride-to-be, with guests bringing recipes for the salads they contribute, and for other favorites, too.

THE SALAD BAR

A number of salad makings are prepared by the hostess in advance and chilled until serving time. Greens, julienne-style vegetables, and strips of meat, poultry, and cheese are some possibilities. Offer a selection of salad dressings, and invite each guest to create her own salad combination.

ACTIVITIES

There are a number of shower customs that are warm expressions of friendship. These traditions are well worth retaining and will keep the shower alive in the bride's memory. While there is no longer the need for a quilting bee, a friendship quilt is a treasure beyond price.

There are other, smaller projects with the personal touch. Buy an unadorned cutting board and ask each guest to write her name or initials on it with a woodburning tool. Or send around a tea towel on which each guest can embroider initials. Put out unhemmed linen towel lengths for guests to hem while visiting. Materials for making paper flowers, and some simple instructions, could start a project that will provide the bride with a centerpiece for her new home.

Such activities go beyond providing a gift for the guest of honor; they give guests a chance to exercise creative talent.

RECIPES FOR A BRIDAL SHOWER

Cranberry Ice

½ cup sugar
1 cup water
1 quart cranberry juice cocktail
1 cup orange juice
½ cup lemon juice
1 quart ginger ale

1. Boil sugar and water together for 5 minutes; cool.
2. Add juices to sugar syrup. Pour into a 3-quart container and put into freezer.
3. When ice crystals begin to form, remove from freezer and stir. Return to freezer.
4. Stir mixture several more times during freezing so it takes on a mushy consistency.
5. Remove from freezer to refrigerator about ½ hour before serving. Stir mixture again at serving time; it should be partly melted. Serve in punch cups.

About 2½ quarts ice

Apple Ice

½ cup sugar
1 cup water
2 cups apple juice
1 cup orange juice
1 tablespoon lemon juice

1. Boil sugar and water 5 minutes; cool.
2. Add juices and freeze. Remove from freezer several times before serving and stir.
3. Serve ice partly frozen in punch cups.

About 1 quart ice

Frozen Fruit Salad

Salad:
    8 ounces cream cheese, softened
    1 can (20 ounces) crushed pineapple, drained (reserve 3 tablespoons syrup)
    ¼ cup mayonnaise
    ½ cup coarsely chopped salted almonds
    ½ cup maraschino cherries, drained and quartered
    ½ cup pitted dates, cut in slivers

1. Blend cream cheese, pineapple syrup, and mayonnaise in a bowl. Mix in crushed pineapple, almonds, maraschino cherries, dates, and marshmallows. Fold in whipped cream. Turn into a 1½-quart mold. Freeze until firm.
2. For dressing, blend the ½ cup of sugar, cornstarch, and salt in the top of a double boiler; stir in ½ cup of the pineapple juice. Over direct heat, bring mixture rapidly to boiling, stirring constantly; cook 2 to 3 minutes. Set over simmering water.
3. Vigorously stir about 3 tablespoons of the hot mixture into the egg yolks in a bowl and immediately blend into

MAY—BRIDAL SHOWERS

24 large marshmallows, cut in eighths
1 cup chilled whipping cream, whipped

Pineapple Salad Dressing:
½ cup sugar
1 tablespoon cornstarch
⅛ teaspoon salt
1½ cups unsweetened pineapple juice
2 egg yolks, slightly beaten
2 egg whites
2 tablespoons sugar
2 tablespoons butter
¾ cup chilled whipping cream, whipped to soft peaks

mixture in double boiler. Cook over simmering water 3 to 5 minutes; stir slowly to keep mixture cooking evenly. Remove double boiler from heat.

4. Beat egg whites until frothy. Add the 2 tablespoons sugar gradually, beating well after each addition. Beat until glossy peaks are formed. Gently blend into the mixture in top of double boiler.

5. Heat the remaining 1 cup pineapple juice to lukewarm. Stirring constantly, gradually add to cooked pineapple-egg white mixture. Cook over simmering water until thick and smooth, stirring constantly, about 10 minutes. Add the butter and stir until melted.

6. Remove from heat and set aside to cool. Set in refrigerator to chill.

7. When pineapple mixture is chilled, gently fold into whipped cream.

8. Serve fruit salad on chilled salad greens with dressing.

8 to 10 servings

Smorgasbord Pear Salads

6 fresh Bartlett pears
Shrimp Filling
Zippy Cheese Filling
Celery-Olive Filling
Salad greens

1. Halve and core pears. Fill 4 halves with Shrimp Filling, 4 with Zippy Cheese Filling, and 4 with Celery-Olive Filling.
2. Arrange filled pears halves on salad greens in a large shallow bowl or on a serving platter.

12 salads

Shrimp Filling: Chop **1 cup cooked deveined shrimp** and combine with **¼ cup chopped celery, 2 tablespoons chopped parsley, 2 teaspoons instant minced onion, ½ teaspoon salt,** and **⅓ cup mayonnaise.**

Zippy Cheese Filling: Combine **1 cup cottage cheese, 1 tablespoon drained capers,** and **1 tablespoon chopped pimento-stuffed olives.**

Celery-Olive Filling: Combine in a small bowl **1 cup cooked sliced celery, ¼ cup ripe olives,** cut in wedges, and **1 tablespoon diced pimento.** Put into a jar with a lid **⅓ cup salad oil, 2 tablespoons vinegar, ½ teaspoon salt,** and **1½ teaspoons sugar;** cover and shake to blend. Pour over celery mixture. Let marinate 2 hours, stirring occasionally.

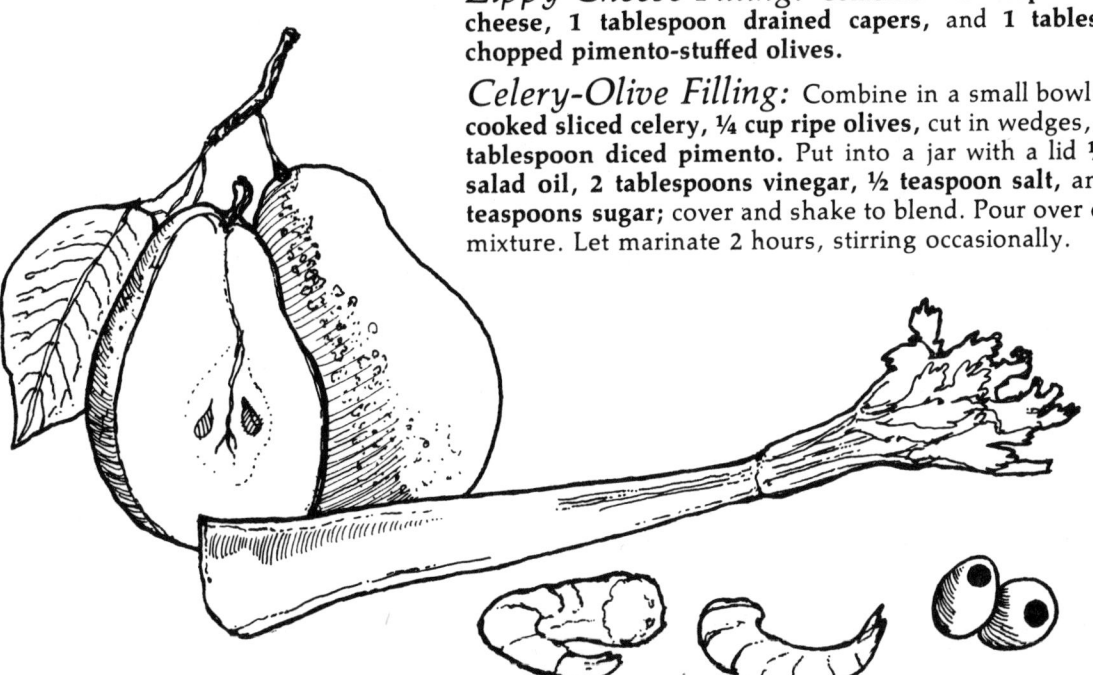

Layered Overnight Salad

- 1 head lettuce, torn in bite-size pieces
- ½ cup chopped onion
- ½ cup chopped celery
- 1 can (5 ounces) water chestnuts, drained and sliced
- 1 package (10 ounces) frozen green peas
- 2 cups mayonnaise
- 1 tablespoon sugar
- 2 large tomatoes, sliced
- 6 hard-cooked eggs, sliced
- ½ pound bacon, cooked and crumbled
- 1 cup grated American cheese food

1. In a 13×9×2-inch dish, make an even layer of the lettuce.
2. Mix onion and celery and sprinkle over.
3. Sprinkle water chestnuts, then unthawed peas over. Spread mayonnaise evenly over top and sprinkle with sugar.
4. Refrigerate overnight.
5. The next day, layer remaining ingredients over mayonnaise.
6. To serve, cut into squares.

12 servings

Salade Niçoise

Salad dressing:
- ½ cup olive oil or salad oil
- 2 tablespoons red wine vinegar
- 1 teaspoon salt
- ½ teaspoon pepper
- 1 teaspoon dry mustard
- 1 tablespoon finely chopped chives
- 1 tablespoon finely chopped parsley

Salad:
- 3 medium-sized cooked potatoes, sliced
- 1 package (9 ounces) frozen green beans, cooked
- 1 clove garlic, cut in half
- 1 small head Boston lettuce
- 2 cans (6½ or 7 ounces each) tuna, drained
- 1 mild onion, quartered and thinly sliced
- 2 ripe tomatoes, cut in wedges
- 2 hard-cooked eggs, quartered
- 1 can (2 ounces) rolled anchovy fillets, drained
- ¾ cup pitted ripe olives
- 1 tablespoon capers

1. For salad dressing, combine olive oil, vinegar, salt, pepper, dry mustard, chives, and parsley in a jar or bottle; shake vigorously to blend well.
2. Pour enough salad dressing over warm potato slices and cooked beans (in separate bowls) to coat vegetables.
3. Before serving, rub the inside of a large shallow salad bowl with the cut surface of the garlic. Line the bowl or a large serving platter with the lettuce.
4. Unmold the tuna in center of bowl and separate into chunks.
5. Arrange separate mounds of the potatoes, green beans, onion, tomatoes, and hard-cooked eggs in colorful groupings around the tuna. Garnish with anchovies, olives, and capers.
6. Pour dressing over all before serving.

6 to 8 servings

Cottage Cheese-Melon Mold

2 packages (16 ounces each) frozen melon balls, thawed and drained (reserve syrup)
2 packages (3 ounces each) lemon-flavored gelatin
2 pounds large-curd creamed cottage cheese, sieved
2 cups whipped cream, whipped to soft peaks
1 cup zwieback crumbs
½ cup sugar
¼ cup finely chopped nuts
¼ cup butter, melted
½ teaspoon freshly grated nutmeg

1. Chop melon balls; set aside.
2. Bring reserved melon syrup to boiling; pour over gelatin in a bowl and stir until gelatin is dissolved. Cool.
3. Stir in 3 cups of the cottage cheese and then the melon balls; fold in whipped cream. Turn into a 9-inch tube pan rinsed with cold water.
4. Mix crumbs, ¼ cup of the sugar, and nuts; blend in melted butter. Sprinkle evenly over top; and press gently. Chill until firm, 6 to 8 hours.
5. Unmold (crumb side will be down).
6. Mix the remaining cottage cheese with a blend of the remaining sugar and nutmeg. Using a pastry bag and star tube, decorate as desired with the flavored cheese.

24 servings

Chicken Salad Polynesian

3 cups cubed cooked chicken meat
Bottled clear French dressing
1 cup chopped celery
1 can (about 8 ounces) crushed pineapple, drained
⅓ cup chopped toasted blanched almonds
¼ cup mayonnaise
Lettuce cups
1 can (11 ounces) mandarin oranges, drained
¼ cup finely cut coconut

1. Coat chicken cubes with French dressing. Refrigerate and marinate several hours or overnight.
2. At serving time, add celery, pineapple, almonds, and mayonnaise; combine well.
3. Serve in lettuce cups and garnish with mandarin oranges and coconut.

6 servings

All-Seasons Macaroni Salad

1 cup dairy sour cream
½ cup Italian salad dressing
½ teaspoon salt
¼ teaspoon seasoned salt
Few grains pepper
2 cups (8 ounces) elbow macaroni, cooked and drained
1½ cups diced cooked chicken
½ pound sliced bacon, panbroiled and crumbled
2 hard-cooked eggs, chopped
¼ cup chopped pimento
1 large tomato, diced
2 tablespoons lemon juice
1 avocado, peeled and sliced
Curly endive

1. Mix together in a bowl the sour cream, salad dressing, and dry seasonings; add macaroni and chicken and mix well. Chill thoroughly.
2. Add bacon, eggs, pimento, and tomato to macaroni; toss lightly. Turn into a salad bowl.
3. Sprinkle lemon juice over avocado slices. Garnish salad with avocado and endive. Additional bacon, chicken, eggs, pimento, and tomato may be used to garnish, if desired.

6 servings

Chicken Mousse

2 envelopes unflavored gelatin
3 cups cold chicken broth
2 tablespoons sweet pickle liquid
1 tablespoon grated onion
1 teaspoon monosodium glutamate
¼ teaspoon salt
¼ teaspoon dry mustard
2½ cups (about 12 ounces) finely chopped cooked chicken or turkey
½ cup finely chopped sweet pickles
½ cup chopped salted blanched almonds
2 cups chilled heavy cream, whipped

1. Soften gelatin in 1 cup of the broth in a saucepan. Stir over low heat until gelatin is dissolved.
2. Mix in remaining broth, pickle liquid, onion, monosodium glutamate, salt, and dry mustard. Chill until mixture is slightly thickened.
3. Fold a mixture of the chicken, pickles, and almonds, and then the whipped cream into the gelatin. Turn into a 2-quart fancy mold. Chill until firm.
4. Unmold onto a chilled serving plate. Garnish with **sweet pickle strips.**

8 to 10 servings

Shrimp and Avocado Salad

1 cup wine vinegar
⅓ cup water
½ cup lemon juice
1 cup salad oil
¼ cup chopped parsley
2 cloves garlic, minced
1 tablespoon salt
¼ teaspoon freshly ground black pepper
1 tablespoon sugar
1 teaspoon dry mustard
1 teaspoon thyme, crushed
1 teaspoon oregano, crushed
2 pounds large shrimp, peeled and deveined
3 small onions, sliced
⅓ cup chopped green pepper
2 ripe avocados, peeled and sliced

1. For marinade, combine vinegar, water, lemon juice, oil, parsley, and garlic in a bowl or a screw-top jar. Add a mixture of salt, pepper, sugar, dry mustard, thyme, and oregano; blend thoroughly.
2. Put shrimp, onions, and green pepper into a large shallow dish. Pour marinade over all, cover, and refrigerate 8 hours or overnight.
3. About 1 hour before serving, put avocado slices into a bowl. Pour enough marinade from shrimp over the avocado to cover completely.
4. To serve, remove avocado slices and shrimp from marinade and arrange on **crisp lettuce** in a large serving bowl.

About 8 servings

Potato Salad Mold

1 envelope unflavored gelatin
¾ cup chicken broth, cooled (dissolve 2 chicken bouillon cubes in ¾ cup boiling water)
2 jars (16 ounces each) mayonnaise-style potato salad
½ cup sliced celery
¼ cup sliced green onions
1 teaspoon garlic salt
1 cup dairy sour cream

1. Sprinkle gelatin over broth in a saucepan to soften. Stir over low heat until gelatin is dissolved. Chill until mixture is slightly thickened.
2. Blend in remaining ingredients. Turn into a 5½-cup ring mold. Chill until firm.
3. Unmold onto a chilled serving plate.

About 8 servings

French Dressings/Creamy, Curried, Lorenzo, Honey, Honey-Lime, Tangy, and Tomato Soup French Dressings

- ¼ cup lemon juice or cider vinegar
- 1 tablespoon sugar
- ¾ teaspoon salt
- ¼ teaspoon paprika
- ¼ teaspoon dry mustard
- ¼ teaspoon pepper
- ¾ cup salad oil or olive oil

Combine all ingredients in a screw-top jar; shake well. Chill. Shake before using.

About 1 cup

Creamy French Dressing: Follow recipe for French Dressing. Blend ¼ cup dairy sour cream with the dressing.

Curried French Dressing: Follow recipe for French Dressing. Mix ¼ teaspoon curry powder with seasonings.

Lorenzo French Dressing: Follow recipe for French Dressing. Add ¼ cup finely chopped watercress and 2 tablespoons chili sauce to the dressing; shake well.

Honey French Dressing: Follow recipe for French Dressing, using lemon juice. Add ½ cup honey and ¼ teaspoon grated lemon peel to dressing and shake well. For added flavor, add ½ teaspoon celery seed and shake well.

Honey-Lime French Dressing: Follow recipe for French Dressing. Substitute ¼ cup lime juice for the lemon juice. Add ½ cup honey and ¼ teaspoon grated lime peel to dressing; shake well.

Tangy French Dressing: Follow recipe for French Dressing. Add 3 to 4 tablespoons prepared horseradish to the dressing and shake well.

Tomato Soup French Dressing: Follow recipe for French Dressing. Add ⅔ cup condensed tomato soup, 1 tablespoon chopped onion, and ½ teaspoon marjoram to the dressing; shake well.

Roquefort Cheese Dressing

- ½ cup Roquefort cheese, crumbled or mashed
- ⅔ cup half-and-half
- 1 teaspoon dry mustard
- ½ teaspoon salt
- ¼ teaspoon pepper
- 1 tablespoon paprika
- ⅔ cup salad oil
- 2 tablespoons lemon juice

1. Blend cheese, half-and-half, dry mustard, salt, pepper, and paprika together in an electric blender or beat in a bowl with a hand rotary beater.
2. Add oil, a tablespoon at a time, beating until thickened and smooth. Beat in lemon juice.
3. Store, covered, in refrigerator.

About 2½ cups

Creamy Lemon-Celery Seed Dressing

1½ cups mayonnaise
¼ cup unsweetened pineapple juice
1 teaspoon grated lemon peel
1 tablespoon lemon juice
½ teaspoon celery seed
Few drops Tabasco

Blend thoroughly mayonnaise, pineapple juice, lemon peel and juice, celery seed, and Tabasco. Cover and refrigerate at least 1 hour to blend flavors.

About 1½ cups

Green Goddess Salad Dressing

1 cup mayonnaise
½ cup dairy sour cream
3 tablespoons tarragon vinegar
1 tablespoon lemon juice
⅓ cup finely snipped parsley
3 tablespoons finely chopped onion
3 tablespoons mashed anchovy fillets
1 tablespoon chopped chives
2 teaspoons chopped capers
1 clove garlic, crushed
⅛ teaspoon salt
⅛ teaspoon pepper

1. Blend all ingredients thoroughly. Cover tightly and chill in refrigerator 3 to 4 hours.
2. To serve, add the dressing to crisp **salad greens** and gently turn and toss until greens are evenly coated. Serve immediately.

About 2½ cups

French Lemon Bars

Cookie crust:
¾ cup butter
1½ cups all-purpose flour
⅓ cup confectioners' sugar
⅛ teaspoon salt

Lemon filling:
3 eggs
1½ cups sugar
3 tablespoons flour
⅓ cup lemon juice

1. For cookie crust, cut butter into flour, sugar, and salt until mixture is crumbly. Press onto the bottom of a 13×9×2-inch pan.
2. Bake at 350°F for 20 minutes.
3. For lemon filling, beat eggs thoroughly in small bowl of electric mixer. Mix sugar and flour, add to eggs and beat well. Add lemon juice and beat until blended.
4. Pour filling over hot crust; return to oven and bake for 20 minutes.
5. Cool; sprinkle lightly with **confectioners' sugar.** Cut into bars.

2 dozen cookies

JUNE
Ice Cream Social

Part of what made the nineties so gay was the ice cream social. On church lawns and in backyard gardens, freezers full of homemade ice cream created more excitement than do today's parlors with their incredible lists of flavors.

You can put some of the nineties gaiety into your June social calendar by having an ice cream social at home. Churches and clubs often organize socials for fund raising. You can have one just for fun raising!

The easiest way to offer a variety of ice cream is to organize your social on the potluck plan. Check with your friends to see who owns an ice cream freezer. Invite each owner to bring a batch of some favorite flavor.

Or you can make all the preparations yourself if you start early enough. Make a flavor each weekend and stock the freezer in readiness.

Vanilla is a must. Don't feel you are shortchanging anyone with vanilla. Commercial sales show it to be the nation's favorite, and it's the basis for so many sundaes, sodas, and other variations.

THE MENU

Right after the ice cream, the items on the most wanted list at any social are the toppers and sauces. Chocolate, butterscotch, strawberry . . . the list is as mouthwatering as it is endless. Put out some fresh fruit, too, including bananas for "splits" fans.

Not to be forgotten at ice cream socials are cakes and cookies. The ice cream should be the star attraction, but it's even better "à la mode" with a choice of baked beauties.

Create a Victorian feeling at your ice cream social, and pick up the nineties theme in the activities you plan. A game of croquet or, if there's room, a bit of horseshoe pitching would be in keeping with the spirit. If someone plays a guitar or banjo, a few songs "by the light of the silvery moon" would set the mood.

But the main order of business will be the enjoyment of ice cream. Here are a few pointers on freezer techniques.

MAKING ICE CREAM

There are recipes for both cooked and uncooked ice cream mixtures. The cooked variety, boasting eggs and cream, is also called "frozen custard." Sometimes flour or cornstarch is added to the custard to help the thickening. Gelatin may be used to thicken uncooked ice cream mixtures.

Ice cream must be stirred continuously during the freezing process, but this is a simple matter with an electric freezer. Stirring is necessary to keep large ice crystals from forming. The smaller the ice crystals, the smoother the finished ice cream. The prevention of large crystals is further aided by adding ingredients such as gelatin, eggs, flour, cornstarch, or rennet.

If the ice cream mixture is cooked before freezing, give it time to cool before pouring it in the freezer can. Fill the can only two-thirds full, since ice cream expands as it freezes. Cover the can and fit it into the freezer. If you are using the electric variety, check the manufacturer's guide for instructions. Pack crushed ice and rock salt alternately around the freezer can in a ratio of eight parts ice to one part rock salt. (Table salt isn't a satisfactory substitute; it causes the ice to melt too quickly.)

If using a hand-operated freezer, turn the crank slowly for about five minutes, to expose as large a surface of the mixture as possible to the cold. When the ice has partially melted, add more ice and salt to maintain the ice level.

After five minutes of slow cranking, or when the mixture is frozen to a mush, the crank should be turned rapidly for about fifteen minutes or until it becomes difficult to turn.

Wipe the lid and remove the dasher. All those helpers who may have faded away will undoubtedly reappear at this point! After a few judicious tastes, pack the ice cream down and cover it with waxed paper. Replace the lid on the can and plug the dasher opening. Repack the freezer container using four parts of crushed ice to one part of rock salt. Cover the freezer with newspapers or heavy cloth and let the ice cream ripen a few hours.

ICE CREAM

Favorite Vanilla Ice Cream/French Vanilla, Chocolate, Chocolate Chip, Buttered Pecan, Berry, and Peach Ice Cream

2 cups milk
1 cup sugar
1 tablespoon flour
¼ teaspoon salt
3 egg yolks, slightly beaten
2 cups cream
2 teaspoons vanilla extract

1. Scald milk in double boiler over simmering water.
2. Combine sugar, flour, and salt; mix well. Add gradually to milk, stirring constantly, and cook over direct heat 5 minutes. Remove from heat and vigorously stir about 3 tablespoons of hot mixture into egg yolks. Immediately stir into hot mixture in top of double boiler. Return to heat and cook over simmering water 10 minutes, stirring constantly until mixture coats a metal spoon. Remove from heat and cool.
3. Stir in cream and vanilla extract. Chill in refrigerator.

For Dasher-Type Freezer: Fill chilled container two-thirds full with ice cream mixture. Cover tightly. Set into freezer tub and, alternating layers, fill with **8 parts crushed ice** and **1 part rock salt.** Turn handle slowly 5 minutes. Turn rapidly until handle becomes very difficult to turn (about 15 minutes). Remove dasher. Pack down ice cream and cover with waxed paper. Put lid on top again and fill opening for dasher with cork. Repack freezer in ice using **4 parts ice** and **1 part rock salt.** Cover with heavy paper or cloth. Let ripen 2 to 3 hours.

For Refrigerator: Pour the chilled mixture into refrigerator trays and place in freezer compartment of refrigerator. When mixture becomes mushy, turn into chilled bowl and beat with chilled rotary beater. This helps to form fine crystals and to give a smooth creamy mixture. Return mixture to trays and freeze until firm.

About 1½ quarts ice cream

French Vanilla Ice Cream: Follow directions for Favorite Vanilla Ice Cream. Omit flour and increase egg yolks to 5. Substitute **2 cups heavy cream** for cream.

Chocolate Ice Cream: Follow directions for Favorite Vanilla Ice Cream. Add **2 ounces (2 squares) unsweetened chocolate** to milk and heat until milk is scalded and chocolate is melted, in top of double boiler.

Chocolate Chip Ice Cream: Follow directions for Favorite Vanilla Ice Cream. Just before freezing, add **2 ounces semi-sweet chocolate**, grated.

Buttered Pecan Ice Cream: Follow directions for Favorite Vanilla Ice Cream. Melt **3 tablespoons butter** in a skillet. Add about **1 cup (about 3¾ ounces) chopped pecans** and heat to golden brown, stirring occasionally. Stir into mixture just before freezing.

Berry Ice Cream: Follow directions for Favorite Vanilla Ice Cream. Just before freezing, blend in **2 cups crushed strawberries or raspberries, sweetened**.

Peach Ice Cream: Follow directions for Favorite Vanilla Ice Cream. Substitute **1 teaspoon almond extract** for vanilla extract. Just before freezing, blend in **1 tablespoon lemon juice** and **1½ cups crushed fresh peaches, sweetened**.

Nectarine Ripple Ice Cream

- 1 cup sugar
- ¾ teaspoon unflavored gelatin
- ⅛ teaspoon salt
- 2 cups half-and-half
- 2 eggs, beaten
- ½ teaspoon vanilla extract
- 1 quart sliced fresh nectarines
- 1 tablespoon lemon juice
- ⅛ teaspoon yellow food coloring
- 2 drops red food coloring
- 1½ cups whipping cream, whipped until stiff

1. Combine ½ cup sugar, gelatin, and salt in a saucepan; mix well. Add half-and-half and heat to scalding over low heat, stirring occasionally. Add the beaten eggs gradually, stirring constantly. Continue to cook 5 minutes over low heat, stirring constantly, until mixture thickens slightly.
2. Remove from heat and stir in vanilla extract; chill.
3. Turn about 1 cup nectarines at a time into an electric blender and blend until particles are very fine, stopping blender and pushing fruit into blades with a rubber spatula. Turn out, then continue blending remainder of nectarines to measure 2 cups. (If blender is not available, cut up fruit and mash fine.) Stir in lemon juice and remaining ½ cup sugar.
4. Stir half of the nectarine mixture and the food coloring into chilled custard. Pour into trays and freeze until firm.
5. Turn frozen mixture into a chilled bowl, break mixture into small chunks, and beat with electric mixer at slow speed until smooth. Fold in whipped cream and return to trays. Set in freezer until almost firm, ½ to 1 hour.
6. Add the remaining nectarines, rippling them in, return to freezer, and freeze until firm.

About ½ gallon ice cream

Cherry Jubilee Ice Cream

- 2 cups fresh dark sweet cherries, rinsed and stems and pits removed
- 1¼ cups sugar
- 1 teaspoon cornstarch
- 1½ cups milk
- 2 eggs
- ½ teaspoon vanilla extract
- ¼ teaspoon lemon extract
- Red food coloring
- 1 cup whipping cream, whipped

1. Finely chop or grind 1 cup cherries. Quarter remaining cherries; set in refrigerator.
2. Combine the sugar and cornstarch in the top of a double boiler; mix well. Add the milk and eggs; beat with hand rotary or electric beater until smooth. Set over boiling water about 10 minutes, stirring constantly. Remove from heat and cool.
3. Stir in the chopped cherries, extracts, and food coloring, a drop at a time, until desired color is obtained. Pour into refrigerator trays and freeze until partially frozen, stirring occasionally.
4. Using a chilled bowl and beater, beat the mixture just until smooth. Fold in the whipped cream and the quartered cherries. Return to trays. Freeze until firm, stirring occasionally.

About 1½ quarts ice cream

Freezer Chocolate Ice Cream

- 1½ cups milk
- 3 ounces (3 squares) unsweetened chocolate
- 1 cup sugar
- ¼ cup flour
- ¼ teaspoon salt
- ½ cup cold milk
- 2 eggs, slightly beaten
- 4 cups whipping cream
- 3 tablespoons vanilla extract

1. Heat milk and chocolate in top of double boiler until milk is scalded and chocolate melted. Set aside.
2. Mix sugar, flour, and salt thoroughly; add cold milk and blend well.
3. Stir sugar mixture into hot milk and chocolate. Stirring constantly, bring rapidly to boiling over direct heat. Cook until mixture is thickened. Place over simmering water and cover; cook 7 minutes, stirring occasionally.
4. Vigorously stir about 3 tablespoons hot mixture into eggs. Immediately return to cooked mixture. Stirring constantly and rapidly, cook 3 to 5 minutes. Remove from heat. Cool.
5. Stir in cream and vanilla extract.

For Dasher-Type Freezer: Fill chilled container two-thirds full with ice cream mixture. Cover tightly. Set in freezer tub. (For electric freezer, follow manufacturer's directions.) Fill tub with alternate layers of **8 parts crushed ice** to **1 part rock salt**. Turn handle slowly 5 minutes. Turn rapidly until handle becomes difficult to turn (about 15 minutes). Wipe lid well and remove dasher. Pack down ice cream and cover with waxed paper. Again put lid on top and fill opening for dasher with cork. Repack freezer container in ice using **4 parts crushed ice** and **1 part rock salt**. Cover with heavy paper or cloth. Let ripen 2 to 3 hours.

For Refrigerator: Pour ice cream mixture into refrigerator trays. When mixture becomes mushy, turn into chilled bowl and beat with chilled beater. Beating helps to form fine crystals and give a smooth, creamy mixture. Return to trays and freeze until firm.

2 quarts ice cream

Philadelphia Ice Cream/Strawberry and Banana Ice Creams

- ¾ cup sugar
- ⅛ teaspoon salt
- 2 cups light cream, scalded
- 1 teaspoon vanilla extract
- 2 cups whipping cream, whipped

1. Stir the sugar and salt into the scalded cream; set aside to cool. Blend in the vanilla extract.
2. Pour mixture into refrigerator trays and freeze until mushy.
3. Remove from freezer and turn into a chilled large bowl. Beat with a rotary beater just until smooth. Fold in the whipped cream. Return to trays and freeze until firm, about 2 hours.

About 2 quarts ice cream

Strawberry Ice Cream: Follow directions for Philadelphia Ice Cream through step 1, omitting vanilla extract. Force **3 cups fresh strawberries** through a food mill; add **¾ cup sugar** to pulp and let stand about 20 minutes. Stir into beaten mixture before first freezing.

Banana Ice Cream: Follow directions for Philadelphia Ice Cream through step 1. Peel **6 all-yellow or brown-flecked bananas.** Force through a sieve or food mill into a bowl. Stir in **1 tablespoon lemon juice.** Stir banana mixture into ice cream before first freezing.

CAKES

Nectarine Chiffon Cake

- 1½ cups sliced unpared fresh nectarines
- 1 tablespoon lemon juice
- 2¼ cups sifted cake flour
- 1½ cups sugar
- 1 tablespoon baking powder
- 1 teaspoon salt
- ½ cup salad oil
- 5 egg yolks (unbeaten)
- 1 teaspoon vanilla extract
- ¼ teaspoon almond extract
- 1 cup egg whites (7 or 8)
- ½ teaspoon cream of tartar

1. Put about half of nectarines at a time into an electric blender container and blend until puréed, stopping blender often and pushing nectarines into blades with a rubber spatula. Turn out into a measuring cup; blend remainder of fruit (should be 1 cup pulp)*. Mix with lemon juice.
2. Sift flour with 1 cup sugar, baking powder, and salt into a mixing bowl. Add oil, egg yolks, nectarine pulp, vanilla and almond extracts to flour mixture; beat to a smooth batter.
3. With clean beaters, beat egg whites with cream of tartar until frothy. Gradually add remaining ½ cup sugar, beating to a stiff meringue; do not underbeat. Pour batter slowly over egg whites, folding in carefully and thoroughly. Turn into an ungreased 10-inch tube pan. Set pan on lowest rack of oven.
4. Bake at 325°F 55 minutes. Turn oven control to 350°F and continue baking 15 minutes, or until a pick inserted in center of cake comes out clean and dry.
5. Invert pan and let cake hang upside down until cooled. Loosen sides and around tube with spatula, and rap pan sharply on counter to remove cake.

One 10-inch tube cake

*If blender is not available, chop nectarines finely so peel is in small pieces, and crush with a fork to obtain moisture needed.

Angel Food Spice Cake

1 cup sifted cake flour
¾ cup sugar
¼ cup cocoa, sifted
1 teaspoon cinnamon
½ teaspoon allspice
½ teaspoon nutmeg
¼ teaspoon cloves
1½ cups egg whites (about 12)
1½ teaspoons cream of tartar
½ teaspoon salt
1 teaspoon vanilla extract
1 cup sugar

1. Sift flour, ¾ cup sugar, cocoa, and spices together and blend thoroughly; set aside.
2. Beat egg whites with cream of tartar, salt, and vanilla extract until stiff, not dry, peaks are formed. Lightly fold in remaining sugar, 2 tablespoons at a time.
3. Gently folding until blended after each addition, sift about 4 tablespoons flour mixture at a time over beaten egg whites. Carefully slide batter into an ungreased 10-inch tube pan. Cut through batter with knife or spatula to break large air bubbles.
4. Bake at 350°F 45 to 50 minutes, or until cake tests done.
5. Immediately invert pan and cool completely. Remove cake from pan. Frost as desired.

One 10-inch tube cake

Triple Chocolate Cake

Cake:
    3 to 4 teaspoons prepared cocoa mix
    ½ cup butter, softened
    ½ cup (4 ounces) cream cheese, softened
    1 teaspoon vanilla extract
    1¼ cups sugar
    2 eggs
    3 cups all-purpose flour
    2 teaspoons baking soda
    1 teaspoon salt
    2 cups milk
    4 ounces (4 squares) unsweetened chocolate, melted

1. For cake, grease three 8-inch round cake pans. Dust with cocoa mix; set aside.
2. Cream butter, cream cheese, vanilla extract, and sugar together until light and fluffy (about 5 minutes). Beat in eggs, one at a time.
3. Stir flour, baking soda, and salt together. Thoroughly blending after each addition, alternately add flour mixture and milk to creamed mixture, beginning and ending with flour.
4. Thoroughly blend melted chocolate into batter. Pour half the batter into prepared pans. Sprinkle fudge pieces evenly over batter in pans. Pour remaining batter into pans.
5. Bake at 350°F 25 minutes, or until a cake tester inserted in cake comes out clean. Cool 10 minutes, then remove from pans. Cool thoroughly before frosting.

1 package (6 ounces) fudge chocolate pieces
Creamy Chocolate Frosting:
1 package (6 ounces) fudge chocolate pieces
1 tablespoon oil
4 ounces cream cheese, softened
⅓ cup butter, softened
4 cups sifted confectioners' sugar
1 teaspoon vanilla extract
1 egg
Milk (about 1 tablespoon)

6. For frosting, melt chocolate pieces with oil.
7. Beat cream cheese and butter together until fluffy. Gradually blend in confectioners' sugar and vanilla extract. Blend in chocolate.
8. Beat in egg; add milk, a teaspoon at a time, until of spreading consistency.
9. Fill and frost cooled layers with frosting.

One 3-layer 8-inch cake

ICE CREAM SAUCES

Chocolate Fudge Sauce

3 ounces (3 squares) unsweetened chocolate
¼ cup butter
⅔ cup sugar
⅛ teaspoon salt
⅔ cup (6-ounce can) evaporated milk
1 teaspoon vanilla extract
Few drops almond extract

1. Melt chocolate and butter in a heavy saucepan over low heat.
2. Remove from heat; stir in sugar and salt until blended. Gradually add evaporated milk, blending well. Cook and stir over low heat until sauce comes to boiling.
3. Remove from heat and stir in extracts. Serve warm.

About 1½ cups sauce

Butterscotch Sauce

1½ cups firmly packed brown sugar
¼ cup water
¼ cup butter

Boil sugar and water together to 234°F, or until a small amount forms a soft ball in cold water. Add butter and stir until melted. Serve warm.

About 1 cup sauce

Nectarine-Pineapple Sundae Sauce

1½ cups pared fresh nectarine slices
1 jar (12 ounces) pineapple sundae topping
¼ teaspoon mint extract or 1 teaspoon rum or brandy extract (optional)

1. If desired, coarsely crush 1 cup of nectarines.
2. Mix nectarines with pineapple topping and, if desired, mint extract.
3. Cover and refrigerate until ready to use.

About 2½ cups sauce

Vanilla Sauce

- 1 cup sugar
- 2 tablespoons cornstarch
- ¼ teaspoon salt
- 2 cups boiling water
- ¼ cup butter or margarine
- 2 teaspoons vanilla extract

1. Mix sugar, cornstarch, and salt thoroughly in a saucepan. Add boiling water gradually, stirring constantly. Continuing to stir, bring to boiling; simmer 5 minutes.
2. Remove from heat and blend in butter and extract. Serve warm or cold.

About 2 cups sauce

Strawberry Sauce

- 2 cups strawberries, rinsed, drained, and hulled
- ½ cup sugar
- 1 tablespoon cold water
- 1½ teaspoons cornstarch

1. Force berries through a sieve or food mill into a saucepan. Blend in sugar and set mixture aside.
2. Make a smooth paste of water and cornstarch. Blend into berry mixture thoroughly. Stirring gently and constantly, bring rapidly to boiling. Continue stirring and boil over medium heat about 3 minutes. Set aside to cool.
3. Cover and chill in refrigerator.

About 1 cup sauce

Lemon Sauce

- 1 cup sugar
- 2 tablespoons cornstarch
- ¼ teaspoon salt
- 2 cups boiling water
- ¼ cup butter or margarine
- 3 tablespoons lemon juice
- 2 teaspoons grated lemon peel

1. Mix sugar, cornstarch, and salt thoroughly in a saucepan.
2. Add boiling water gradually, stirring constantly. Continuing to stir, bring to boiling; simmer 5 minutes.
3. Remove from heat and blend in butter, lemon juice, and grated lemon peel. Serve warm or cold.

About 2 cups sauce

Walnut Praline Sauce

- ¼ cup butter, softened
- ¼ cup firmly packed light brown sugar
- ¾ cup light corn syrup
- ¾ cup chopped walnuts
- 2 tablespoons water

1. Cream butter and brown sugar together in a medium-size saucepan. Stir in syrup and nuts.
2. Cook over medium heat, stirring constantly, until mixture comes to a full boil; then boil 3 minutes, or until mixture reaches 234°F on a candy thermometer.
3. Remove from heat and stir in water. Serve warm over ice cream.

About 1½ cups sauce

JULY Cookout

Some men can be lured into cooking through the back door—especially if there's a bed of coals and a juicy steak waiting. Outdoor cooking has probably won more men over to cooking than has any other inducement.

So make your July party a cookout, and chances are good that you can count on Dad for help. Out on the patio or at the park, there's no way that too many cooks can spoil the broth—or the chief chef's disposition. In fact, the more the merrier. He'll welcome all the help he can get to line up ingredients, peel and chop, and handle the rest of the details while he takes honors at grillside.

FOOD

Since there's so much fresh air fun to be had, keep the July cookout simple. A few easy innovations will make the menu a party meal. Either Sauce-Painted Spareribs or Barbecued Beef Chuck Steak will make a popular headliner.

Or if you're having a backyard picnic, combine indoor with outdoor cooking. Prepare the accompaniments on the grill, while broiling a Marinated Onion-Topped Burger Loaf inside.

A day or two ahead of the cookout prepare a special sauce or topping to add party flair to grill fare. Onion Confetti Relish, or any of the barbecue sauces could perform the party magic.

DECORATIONS

You can have a successful cookout without a thought to table setting. But if yours is to be a party, even if it's just for family, add a few bright touches to the table.

Decorations needn't be expensive. You can make an easy tablecloth from an unpretentious plastic leaf bag. Cut down one side and across the bottom of the bag, and lay it out flat on the picnic table. If there are willing hands to help, let them decorate the tablecloth with designs cut from adhesive backed paper.

Another large plastic bag will make a he-man-sized apron for Pop. Leave the bag double, and cut an apron shape (page 54). Reinforce the cut edges with tape. Baste a two-yard length of ribbon across the waist, leaving ends to tie in back.

Leaf bags can even provide entertainment while dinner cooks. Have on hand long wood dowels, knives, scissors, glue, and balls of cord. Help the little ones make kite frames by using cord to lash together two dowels. The vertical dowel should be longer than the horizontal one. Notch the ends of the dowels and run heavy cord through the four notched ends. Pull the cord taut so the frame bows, and tie the cord at the bottom, leaving some length for the kite tail. Cut a leaf bag about two inches wider than the outline of cord running between the dowels. Fold the outer two inches of plastic over the cord and glue down the edges. Tie a few plastic strips cut from the leaf bag to the tail of the kite. Attach the ball of cord to the point where the dowels cross, as illustrated.

The job is done—now go fly a kite!

GETTING READY TO BARBECUE

The guy at the grill will have more serious matters on his mind. He'll be getting the grill ready for the meat of the meal.

Lay the groundwork for that bed of coals by lining the brazier with heavy-duty foil. This helps at cooking time by reflecting heat back onto the food, and at cleanup time when it is tossed out.

On the foil, spread a shallow layer of sand or gravel before adding the briquets. This layer catches dripping fat and reduces flare-ups. Get the coals going by piling them into a two-pound can from which the ends have been removed and holes punched around the bottom. Stand this homemade chimney in the firebox of your grill, sprinkle on liquid fire starter, and light the coals by placing a match through one of the punched holes.

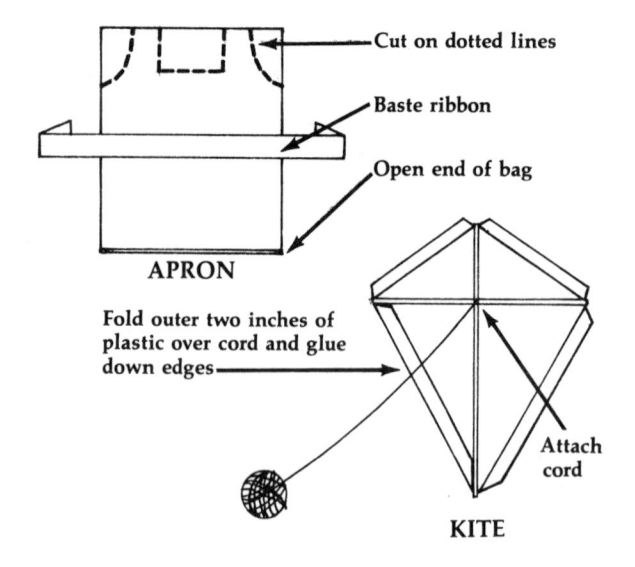

Allow the coals to burn fifteen or twenty minutes, use tongs to remove the chimney, and rake the coals out into the firebox. Wait until the fire is reduced to glowing coals before cooking, usually around a half hour.

MAIN DISHES FROM THE GRILL

Barbecued Beef Chuck Steak

1 beef chuck steak (1½ pounds), 1½ inches thick
½ cup chutney
3 tablespoons lemon juice
⅓ cup ketchup
   Salt and pepper

1. Trim fat from edges of beef. Put steak into a shallow pan.
2. Combine chutney, lemon juice, and ketchup in an electric blender; blend until smooth.
3. Pour chutney mixture over steak. Turn to coat both sides. Allow to stand an hour or longer.
4. Drain steak well and reserve marinade.
5. Grill steak over charcoal, sprinkling with salt and pepper. Grill 10 minutes on each side, or until a small cut near the center of steak shows the color you desire.
6. Heat remaining marinade and serve as sauce. Slice steak in diagonal strips to serve.

4 servings

Sauce-Painted Spareribs

4 pounds pork spareribs or back ribs, cut in serving portions
1 cup ketchup
¼ cup lemon juice
2 tablespoons brown sugar
1 tablespoon soy sauce

1. Partially cook ribs in a large pan with a rack in a 350°F oven about 30 minutes.
2. Meanwhile, combine remaining ingredients in a saucepan. Simmer over low heat at least 10 minutes. Remove garlic.
3. To grill, place ribs, meaty side down, on grill. Slowly grill

- 1 tablespoon prepared horseradish mustard
- 1 tablespoon grated onion
- 1½ teaspoons salt
- ½ teaspoon pepper
- ¼ teaspoon oregano, marjoram, or thyme
- ¼ teaspoon Tabasco
- 1 clove garlic

about 3 inches from coals. Turn about every 5 minutes, brushing with sauce. Grill until ribs are deep brown and crisp, about 25 minutes.

8 servings

Marinated Onion-Topped Burger Loaf

- 1 medium sweet Spanish onion
- ½ cup clear French dressing
- 1 tablespoon chopped parsley
- ¾ pound ground beef
- 1 teaspoon pepper
- ¼ teaspoon garlic salt
- 1 teaspoon Worcestershire sauce
- French bread
- Prepared mustard
- 4 slices American cheese, cut crosswise in triangles

1. Peel and thinly slice onion. Separate into rings. Combine French dressing with chopped parsley and marinate onion rings.
2. Combine ground beef and seasonings.
3. Cut French bread in half lengthwise. Spread bottom half with desired amount of prepared mustard. Spread ground beef filling evenly over surface. Place under broiler and broil until meat is done as desired. Toast cut side of top half.
4. Arrange cheese triangles on top of hamburger. Place under broiler again until cheese melts.
5. Drain onion rings and arrange over cheeseburger filling. Put top on loaf. To serve, cut into crosswise slices.

About 4 servings

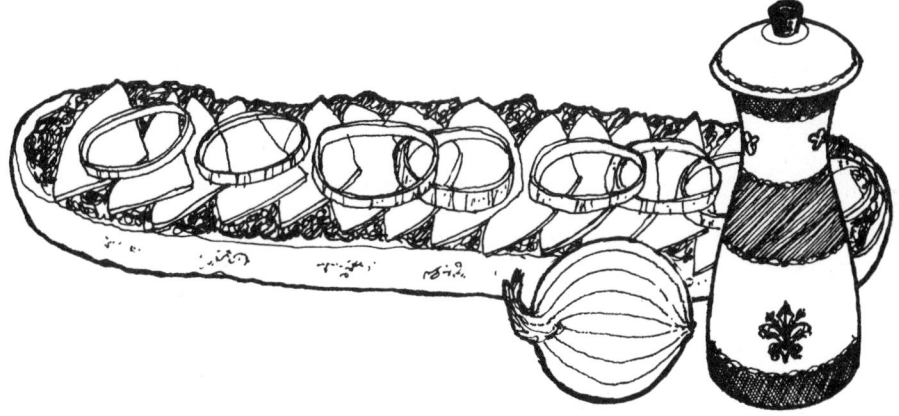

SAUCES AND ACCOMPANIMENTS

Peppy Barbecue Sauce

- ½ pound butter or margarine
- 2 small onions, finely chopped
- 1 cup ketchup
- ½ cup Worcestershire sauce
- 1½ teaspoons sugar
- 1 teaspoon dry mustard
- 1 clove garlic, minced
- 1½ cups water
- 1 cup vinegar
- Juice of 1 lemon

1. Melt butter in large skillet. Add onion and cook 2 minutes.
2. Add ketchup, Worcestershire sauce, sugar, dry mustard, and garlic; stir well.
3. Add water, vinegar, and lemon juice. Simmer ½ hour. May be made in advance and stored in refrigerator.

About 1 quart sauce

Barbecue

	Preparation	Distance from Coals	Cooking & Timing
BEEF			
STEAKS	Slash fat to prevent curling. If desired, soak in marinade several hours or overnight.	3 inches (1-inch steaks) 5 inches (2-inch steaks)	Grill 6 to 10 minutes on each side for rare; 12 to 15 minutes for medium. Season and brush with sauce after grilling. To see if done, cut slit and check color.
RIB ROAST	Run rotisserie spit through center of meat lengthwise. Balance evenly. Fasten with holding forks. Attach spit and turn on motor. Have hot coals at back of firebox and drip pan under roast.	On rotisserie	About 2 hours for medium-rare for 5-pound roast, or until meat thermometer shows 140°F for rare, 160°F for medium, or 170°F for well-done.
BURGERS	Place 1-inch thick patties in a hinged basket broiler or on a greased grill.	4 to 5 inches	5 minutes on each side. When brown, season and turn. If using sauce, brush frequently.
KABOBS	Soak in marinade. Thread on skewers; place close together for rare or separate for well done.	3 inches	15 to 20 minutes, turning and brushing frequently with marinade.
PORK			
SPARERIBS	Place on rack in shallow pan; add salt and pepper. Cover with foil. Bake in 350°F oven 30 minutes. Transfer to grill.	6 to 8 inches	40 to 50 minutes, turning frequently and brushing with barbecue sauce.
HAM SLICES	Place on grill over hot coals.	4 to 5 inches	5 minutes on each side, brushing frequently with sauce, if desired.
FRANKS	Place in basket broiler or on grill.	3 inches	2 or 3 minutes on each side.
CANADIAN BACON ROLL OR SMOKED SHOULDER ROLL	Secure meat on spit; follow manufacturer's directions for rotisserie.	Rotisserie	About 1½ hours, or until medium for 1½-pound roll, or until meat thermometer registers 170°F. Brush frequently with sauce.
LAMB			
CHOPS (loin, rib, or shoulder)	Trim excess fat, marinate if desired and place on grill.	4 inches	Thickness — Minutes/side ¾ inch — 10 to 12 1 inch — 14 to 16 1½ inches — 16 to 18 2 inches — 20 to 22
KABOBS	Soak in marinade, if desired. Thread cubes on skewers; close for rare, separate for well-done.	4 inches	15 to 20 minutes. Cut a small slit to check color.

Basics

	Preparation	Distance from Coals	Cooking & Timing
PATTIES	Wrap bacon around lamb patties. Secure with wooden picks.	4 to 6 inches	5 minutes on each side.

POULTRY

	Preparation	Distance from Coals	Cooking & Timing
WHOLE BIRDS (Rock Cornish hens, ducks, chickens, turkeys)	Rinse; pat dry. Season body cavity. Fasten neck skin to back with skewer. Tie, using at least 2 feet of cord. Start at back and bring cord forward, tying wings flat to breast. Tie drumsticks securely to tail. Insert spit through center of bird from breast to tail. Insert holding forks into breast meat. Brush with oil. Baste with sauce last 30 minutes of cooking time.	Rotisserie	Depends on size of bird. Cornish hen: 1 to 1½ hours. Chicken: 2 hours. Duck: 2 hours. Turkey: 15 minutes per pound or until drumstick moves easily. Or until thickest part of drumstick feels soft when pressed. Meat thermometer should register 190°F.
HALVES, QUARTERS, OR PIECES	Fold wing tips toward cut side. Brush with oil or barbecue sauce.	5 inches	20 minutes first side; turn. Grill 20 minutes longer, or until meat shows no pink color when slit is cut.

FISH

	Preparation	Distance from Coals	Cooking & Timing
LOBSTER— LIVE	Place on cutting board. Kill quickly by inserting point of sharp, heavy knife in center of small cross on the back of the head. Without removing knife, quickly bear down heavily, cutting through entire length of body and tail. Split halves; remove stomach, a small sac lying in the head, and the spongy lungs lying between meat and shell. Also remove dark intestinal line running through center of body. Crack large claws with mallet. Brush with seasoned butter. Place shell side down on grill.	5 inches	About 20 minutes or until shell is browned, basting frequently with seasoned butter.
LOBSTER— ROCK LOBSTER TAILS	Thaw frozen lobster tails. Cut around under-shell and remove. Insert skewer lengthwise through meat to keep tail flat. Brush with butter sauce.	4 inches	7 minutes
SHRIMP	Cut each raw shrimp through shell along back. Remove black vein. Carefully spread shell open; rinse and drain. Marinate. Grill in hinged basket broiler 1 layer deep.	3 inches	15 minutes

Side Dishes from the Grill

	Preparation	Distance from Coals	Cooking & Timing
ROAST CORN	Loosen husks just enough to remove silks and blemishes. Shake well. Rewrap husks around ears; soak in water about 1 hour. Place on grill with stem ends extending beyond edge of grill.	4 to 6 inches	Roast about 15 minutes, or until tender, turning often. Husk and serve with butter.
BAKED POTATOES	Wash, scrub, dry. Rub on fat and wrap each potato in foil. Seal ends with double fold.	4 to 6 inches	Bake 1 hour, or until soft when pressed. Turn several times for even baking.
GRILLED TOMATOES	Cut into halves crosswise. Brush with melted butter; season. Place on grill, cut side up.	4 to 6 inches	Grill about 3 minutes.
GRILLED ONIONS	Leave outside skins on. Wet thoroughly; place on grill. Roll onions occasionally while grilling.	4 to 6 inches	Grill about 50 minutes, or until black on outside and soft and creamy on inside.
RATATOUILLE IN PACKETS	For each serving, place on pieces of heavy-duty foil layers of eggplant, onion, tomato, and zucchini slices. Season with garlic salt, basil, and pepper to taste. Pour over each 1 teaspoon olive oil. Fold packets, seal ends with double fold.	4 to 6 inches	Cook 30 minutes, turning several times.
GARLIC BREAD	Make diagonal slices in French bread almost through loaf. Spread with garlic-seasoned butter. Wrap loaf loosely in foil, sealing ends with double fold.	4 to 6 inches	Heat 10 minutes, turning frequently.
BAKED APPLES IN FOIL	For each serving, core apple; pare 1-inch strip around top. Fill cavity with raisins and nuts. Place on large piece of heavy-duty foil. Pour equal parts orange juice and honey (about 1 tablespoon liquid) over each apple. Seal in foil, making double fold at ends. Place on grill.	3 inches	Bake about 1 hour or until tender.
TOASTED MARSH-MALLOWS	Spear on long forks or sticks; hold over grill.	3 inches	Toast 1 or 2 minutes, turning often. Sandwich between graham crackers with candy bar squares for "S'Mores."

Lemon Barbecue Sauce

1 small clove garlic
½ teaspoon salt
¼ cup salad oil
½ cup lemon juice
2 tablespoons chopped onion
½ teaspoon black pepper
½ teaspoon dried thyme

1. Mash garlic clove with salt in a bowl.
2. Stir in remaining ingredients. Allow sauce to stand at least 1 hour to blend flavors.

About ¾ cup sauce

Herb Barbecue Sauce

1 small onion
3 cloves garlic
2 sprigs rosemary (or 1 teaspoon dried rosemary)
12 fresh mint leaves (or 1 teaspoon dried mint leaves)
½ cup vinegar
½ cup water

1. Chop onion and garlic fine.
2. Add rosemary and mint leaves which have been crushed.
3. Add vinegar and water; stir well. Let mixture stand 4 to 6 hours.

About 1 cup sauce

Butter Sauce

1 cup butter
2 tablespoons lemon juice
¼ teaspoon salt
¼ teaspoon paprika
⅛ teaspoon black pepper
¼ cup chopped parsley

In a small saucepan combine all ingredients. Heat until butter is melted.

About 1 cup sauce

Orange Butter Sauce

1 can (6 ounces) frozen orange juice concentrate (undiluted)
¼ cup lemon juice
½ teaspoon dry mustard
¼ teaspoon rosemary
½ teaspoon celery salt
½ teaspoon onion powder
½ teaspoon salt
¼ teaspoon Angostura bitters
½ cup butter or margarine

Combine all ingredients in a saucepan; heat slowly, stirring constantly, until mixture comes to a boil; boil 1 minute.

About 1½ cups sauce

Sweet-Sour Apricot Sauce

- 2 cans (30 ounces each) apricot halves, drained
- ½ cup drained crushed pineapple
- ½ cup honey
- ½ cup brown sugar
- ½ teaspoon salt
- Few grains white pepper
- 2 tablespoons cider vinegar
- 2 large cloves garlic, quartered

1. Force apricots through a sieve or food mill into a saucepan. Stir in a mixture of pineapple, honey, brown sugar, salt, white pepper, and vinegar, then garlic.
2. Bring mixture to boiling, reduce heat to medium, and cook 10 minutes, stirring occasionally. Remove garlic. Cool and store, covered, in refrigerator until ready to use.

About 2½ cups sauce

Savory Onion Topper

- 3 cups chopped sweet Spanish onion
- 3 tablespoons butter
- 1¼ cups chili sauce
- ¼ cup bottled meat sauce

1. Sauté onion in butter in a skillet until tender. Mix in chili sauce and meat sauce; heat thoroughly.
2. Serve over grilled or broiled hamburgers.

About 2½ cups sauce

Onion Confetti Relish

- 2 cups chopped sweet Spanish onion (1 large)
- ½ green pepper, diced
- 3 tablespoons diced pimento
- ½ cup vinegar
- ¼ cup water
- ¼ cup sugar
- 2 teaspoons caraway seed
- ½ teaspoon salt

1. Combine onion with green pepper and pimento.
2. Combine vinegar, water, sugar, caraway seed, and salt. Bring to boiling and simmer 5 minutes. Pour over onion mixture. Refrigerate several hours.
3. Serve with grilled or broiled hamburgers.

2½ cups relish

Crispy French Fried Onion Rings

- 2 sweet Spanish onions
- 1 cup pancake mix
- ¾ cup beer
- Oil for deep frying heated to 375°F
- Salt

1. Peel onions and cut into ½ inch thick slices; separate into rings.
2. Combine pancake mix and beer to make a smooth, thick batter.
3. Dip onion rings in batter and fry, a few at a time, in hot fat until golden brown. Drain on absorbent paper lined baking sheets.
4. Keep fried onion rings hot in oven until all rings are fried.

Note: To freeze fried onion rings, leave onion rings on lined baking sheets, place in freezer, and freeze quickly. Then carefully remove rings to moisture-vaporproof containers with layers of absorbent paper between layers of onions. Cover container tightly and freeze. To heat frozen onion rings, place rings on a baking sheet and heat in a 375°F oven for several minutes.

AUGUST
Posh Picnics

Most picnics are pick-up-and-go, but come August you may be ready for a change of pace. Treat yourself to one midsummer night's dream of a feast under the stars. A beautifully set table topped with a banquet of chilled dishes will create an effect worthy of the work.

Set up your elegant picnic in your own backyard or go to some attractive setting farther afield. Just so it's out of doors and out of context with the usual, expected picnic. There should be an effect of sleight of hand, as if all that elegance had just appeared, by magic!

In order to accomplish this, you'll need to lay the groundwork early. The more time and thought you give, the more serene will be the picnic itself.

THE MENU

Although it's possible to carry hot dishes to the picnic site in insulated containers, they are more trouble, and extra care must be taken to avoid food spoilage.

Take the simpler route and plan an all-chilled menu. It's bound to please on a warm evening, anyway. Main dish candidates include meat loaves that can be baked, then chilled. Our ham loaf in a brioche jacket has the right touch of class for this affair.

Other meats, fish, and poultry that can be cooked and chilled in advance are possibilities. Consider glazing a large whole cooked fish, perhaps a salmon or trout. Glaze and decorate the fish with slices of stuffed olives, anchovies, or beets. Or if the sky is truly the limit for this open-air affair, splurge on truffles.

You might also serve layers of sliced cooked meat in aspic. Give the decorative flourishes to the bottom of the aspic mold before the meat goes in, since it will become the crown when you unmold the dish at the picnic site.

A chilled herbed vegetable platter is an attractive partner for the main dish. Choose vegetables that offer color contrast, such as baby carrots, green beans, cauliflower, and fresh mushrooms. After cooking, the vegetables are marinated in an herb salad dressing.

Fruit salad is a colorful stroke. Rings cut from cantaloupe and filled with blueberries taste as good as they look. A watermelon boat takes a little time to carve, but it does double duty as both centerpiece and salad or dessert. Fresh pineapples, split, carved, and filled with a fruit compote serve the same purpose.

Choose a bread for your spread that doesn't depend on being hot to be interesting. Salted bread sticks, crusty French rolls, and Melba toast are all fine.

If fruit hasn't already appeared in the menu, a compote makes a satisfying dessert. Or try

AUGUST—POSH PICNICS

Sherry-Coconut Chiffon Cake. It travels well, and having only a confectioners' sugar dusting rather than a frosting, it's not messy to handle.

THE WINE

Wine belongs at this picnic. In fact, you might hold a wine tasting as prelude to the feast itself, allowing you more time to get things arranged and providing diversion for your guests.

A simple wine tasting can be built around one type of wine, such as a rosé, a favorite in summertime. Select three different brands, all from California, or perhaps a combination of domestic and imported rosés. Before serving, chill the wines well. Ask your guests to note differences in color, sweetness, and flavor. If this is a get-acquainted-with-rosé tasting, there is no need to hide labels.

Another type of wine tasting is more of a challenge. Offer three bottles of wine, two of them identical—say, pinot noir—and the third bottle a zinfandel. The object is to identify the odd one.

The equipment for the tasting is simple. In addition to the wines provide some means of disguising the bottles. Colorful bags work nicely. Only one glass per guest is necessary. There are many parties, both professional and private, that are known as one-glass tastings, and for a picnic it is simplest.

During the wine tasting, the only food you need offer are cubes of French bread to clear the palate. Sometimes cubes of mild cheese are added to the tray.

THE TABLE SETTING

Along with the menu, it's the table setting that will make your picnic posh. Appointments that are city slick seem even more sophisticated in a sylvan setting.

If you want to use your best china and crystal, pack them with care. Or take second-best dishes and rely on your best silver serving pieces and candelabra—all unbreakable—for the fancy touches. Paperware would really break the mood. For this special outing take a lace or linen cloth and napkins.

TIMING

Elegant picnics belong at the end of the day, just as dusk arrives to add to the enchantment. But don't start your evening too late. Even with candlelight, it's difficult to serve after dark.

Under-the-stars dining often leads into another event such as an outdoor concert. A menu such as any of these will put your crowd in a receptive mood.

WINE TASTING PICNIC

California Red, White, or Rosé Dinner Wine Tasting

Ham Loaf in a Jacket

Tossed Green Salad

Sherry-Coconut Chiffon Cake

Fresh Fruit

Ham Loaf in a Jacket

Brioche Dough:
- 1 package (13¾ ounces) hot roll mix
- ¼ cup warm water
- ⅓ cup milk

1. For brioche dough, combine yeast from packet in hot roll mix with warm water.
2. Scald milk and cool to lukewarm.
3. Cream butter and sugar. Add eggs and yeast; mix well. Stir in flour mixture from mix alternately with milk, beating

⅓ cup butter or margarine
2 tablespoons sugar
3 eggs, beaten

Ham Loaf:
2 cups ground cooked ham
1 pound ground veal or lean beef
2 eggs, beaten
2 cups fine soft bread crumbs
¾ cup California Sauterne
½ teaspoon dry mustard
½ teaspoon salt
¼ teaspoon pepper
½ cup coarsely chopped ripe olives
¼ cup diced pimento
1 tablespoon instant minced onion

until smooth after each addition. Cover tightly; let rise in a warm place until light, about 1 hour. Stir down and set in refrigerator until thoroughly chilled.
4. Meanwhile, prepare ham loaf.
5. For ham loaf, combine all ingredients and mix well. Turn into a greased fluted brioche pan, about 8½ inches across top and about 1-quart capacity; pack into pan and round up center.
6. Bake at 350°F 1 hour. Cool in pan about 10 minutes, then turn out of pan and cool thoroughly.
7. Divide chilled brioche dough in half. Roll each portion into a round about 10 inches in diameter. Turn cooled ham loaf up side down and fit a round of dough over bottom and sides. Trim off excess dough. Holding dough in place, quickly invert loaf and fit other round of dough over top and sides. Trim edges evenly.
8. Place dough-wrapped loaf in well-greased brioche pan a size larger than one used for ham loaf, about 9½ inches in diameter across top and about 2-quarts capacity.
9. Shape dough trimmings into a ball and place on top of loaf. Let rise in warm place about 30 to 45 minutes, or until dough is light.
10. Set on lowest shelf of 375°F oven. Bake 10 to 15 minutes, or until top is browned. Place a piece of brown paper or aluminum foil over top of loaf. Continue baking about 25 minutes, or until nicely browned and baked through (test brioche with wooden pick).
11. Turn loaf out of pan and serve warm or cold, cut in wedges.

About 8 servings

Sherry-Coconut Chiffon Cake

2 cups sifted all-purpose flour
1½ cups sugar
1 tablespoon baking powder
1 teaspoon salt
⅔ cup cooking oil
2 egg yolks
½ cup water
¼ cup California Sherry or Muscatel
2 teaspoons vanilla extract
½ cup flaked coconut
1 cup egg whites (7 or 8)
½ teaspoon cream of tartar
Confectioners' sugar (optional)

1. Sift flour, 1 cup sugar, baking powder, and salt into a bowl. Make a well and add, in order, oil, egg yolks, water, sherry, and vanilla extract. Beat to a smooth batter. Mix in coconut.
2. Pour egg whites into a very large mixing bowl. Sprinkle cream of tartar over egg whites. Whip until soft peaks are formed. Add remaining ½ cup sugar gradually, beating until very stiff peaks are formed. Do not underbeat (whites should be stiffer than for angel food cake or meringue).
3. Pour batter slowly over whites, gently folding with rubber spatula or large spoon just until blended.
4. Turn immediately into an ungreased 10×4-inch tube pan.
5. Bake at 325°F 1 hour and 10 minutes, or until top surface springs back when lightly touched with finger and the cracks look dry.
6. Remove from oven and turn upside down. Cool completely in pan.
7. Loosen cake from sides and center tube. Turn pan over and hit edge sharply on table to loosen.
8. Put cake on a serving plate. If desired, sift confectioners' sugar over top.

One 10-inch tube cake

BEFORE THE CONCERT AFFAIR

Glazed Decorated Salmon

Soufflé Mont Blanc

Roquefort-Vegetable Salad

Zucchini Bread (for cream cheese finger sandwiches)

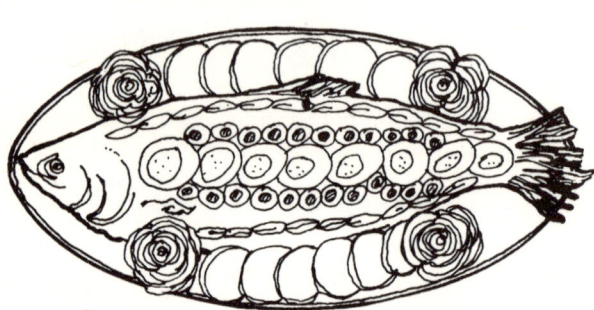

Carved Watermelon Boat

Glazed Decorated Salmon

- 2 cups dry white wine, such as sauterne
- 2 cups water
- 1 onion
- 1 carrot, sliced
- 1 celery stalk, sliced
- 1 clove garlic, sliced
- 1 bay leaf
- 1 teaspoon crushed thyme
- 1 teaspoon salt
- ⅛ teaspoon pepper
- 1 whole cleaned salmon (about 4 pounds) or other whole fish
- 1 slightly beaten egg white and shell
- 2 envelopes unflavored gelatin
- ½ cup dry white wine, such as sauterne
- 1 hard-cooked egg, sliced
  Pimento-stuffed olives, sliced
  Mayonnaise (optional)

1. For court bouillon, combine 2 cups wine, water, vegetables, and seasonings in a fish poacher or large shallow pan. Simmer, covered, 10 minutes.
2. Place whole fish in court bouillon. Cook, covered, 10 minutes. Allow fish to cool in liquid. Remove fish and chill.
3. Strain court bouillon into a saucepan. Add egg white and shell. Boil 2 minutes. Cool and strain through a double thickness of cheesecloth.
4. Soften gelatin in ½ cup wine. Add to court bouillon and heat until gelatin dissolves. Chill until mixture starts to set.
5. Cover the bottom of a cold platter with thickened gelatin. Arrange salmon on it. Spoon some of the gelatin mixture over salmon and decorate with slices of hard-cooked egg and stuffed olive. Let stand until set.
6. Spoon more gelatin over garnish. Chill again until firm. Pour remaining gelatin into a shallow pan and chill until firm.
7. At serving time, cut gelatin in pan into diamonds or other fancy shapes to garnish platter.
8. If desired, pipe mayonnaise onto glazed fish for a final touch. Also, garnish platter with crisp lettuce hearts and slices of hard-cooked egg and pickled beets or truffles.

About 8 servings

Ham Loaf in a Jacket;
Sherry-Coconut Chiffon Cake

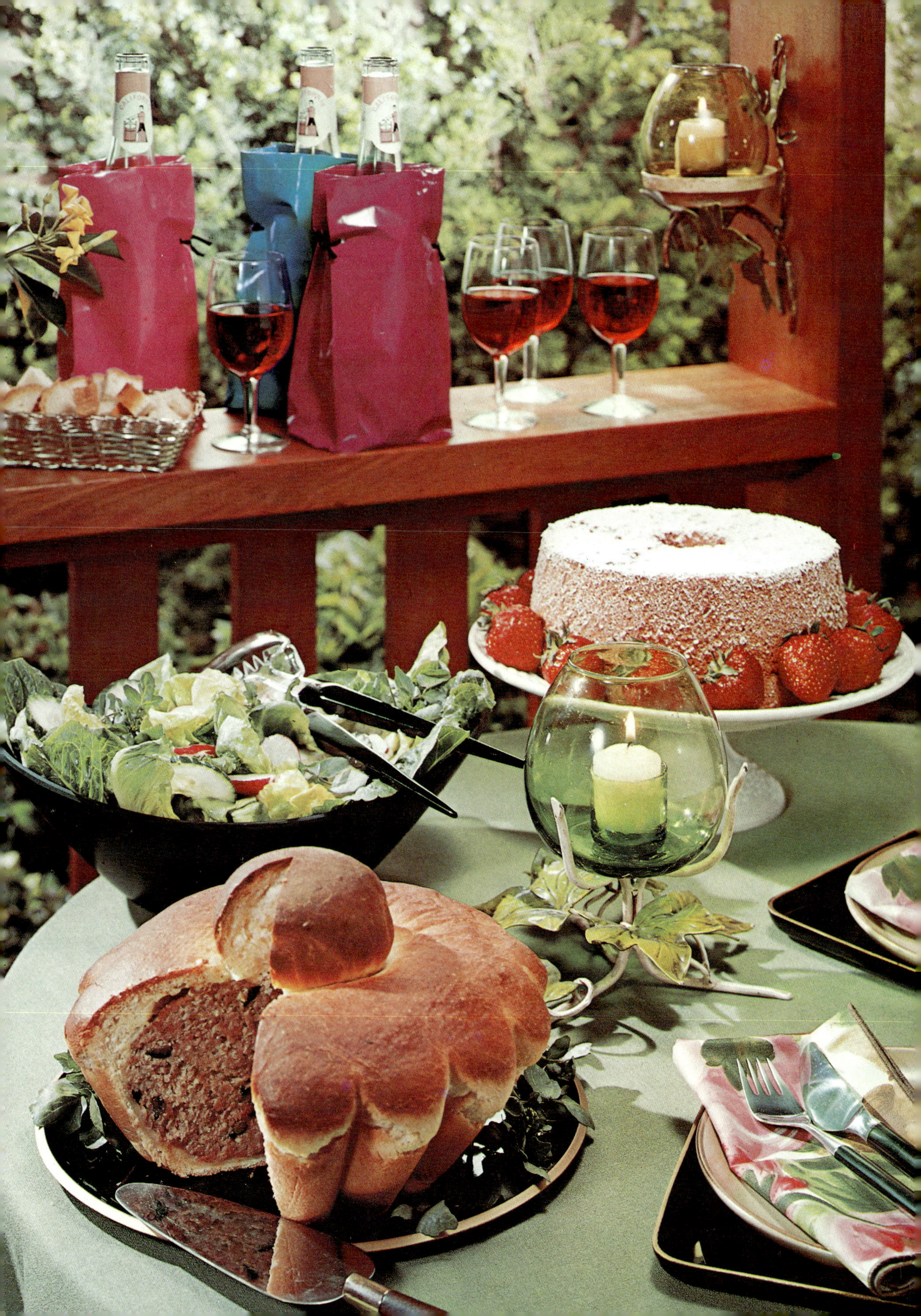

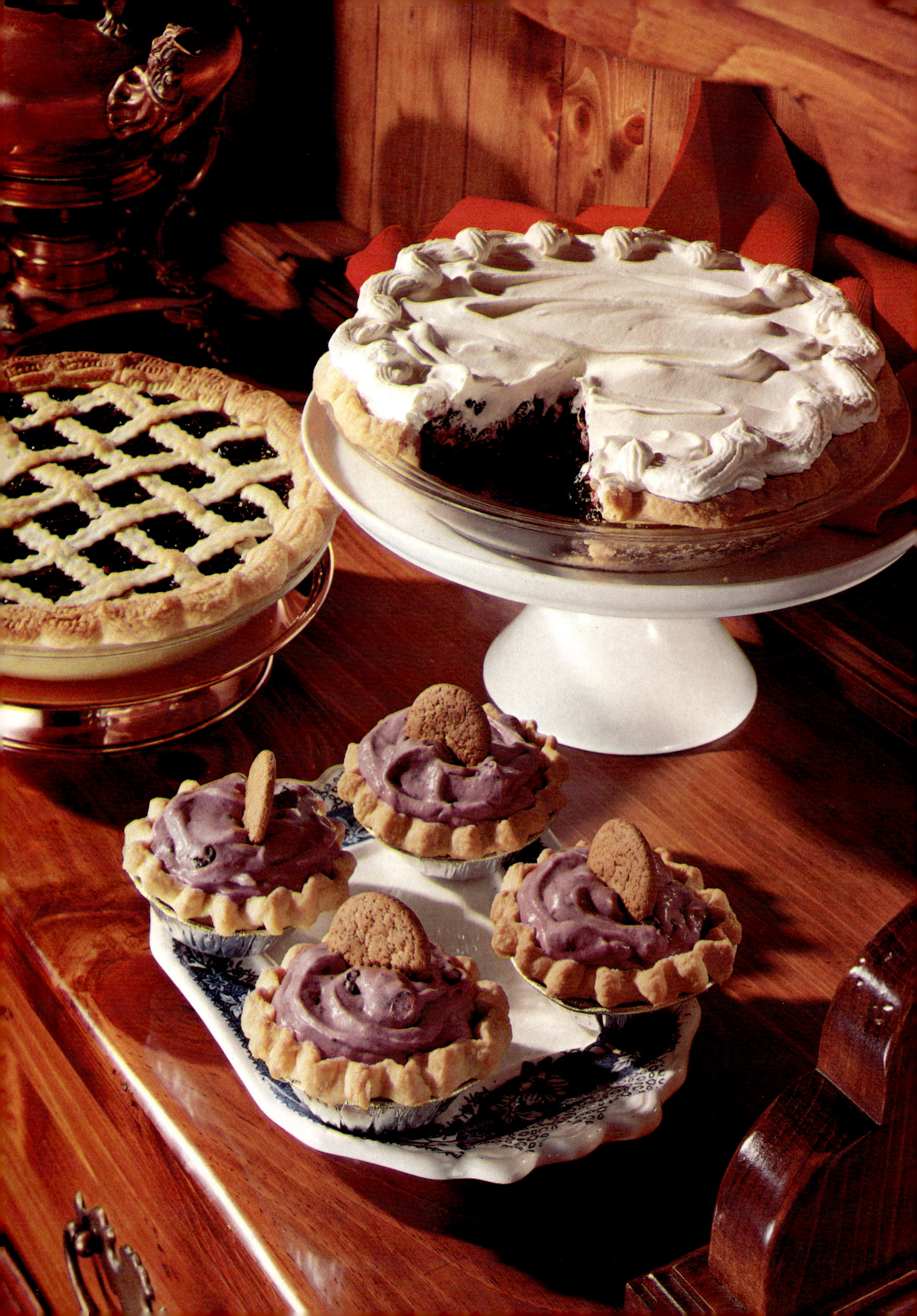

Soufflé Mont Blanc

1 envelope unflavored gelatin
½ cup milk
¼ cup water
1 teaspoon lemon juice
1 teaspoon grated onion
　Few drops Tabasco
½ teaspoon salt
¼ teaspoon dry mustard
2 cups finely shredded Parmesan cheese
2 cups chilled whipping cream, whipped

1. Sprinkle gelatin evenly over milk and water in a saucepan. Stir over low heat until gelatin is dissolved.
2. Blend lemon juice, onion, Tabasco, and a mixture of salt and dry mustard into dissolved gelatin; stir in cheese. Fold with whipped cream. Turn mixture into a 1½-quart mold. Chill until firm.
3. Unmold onto a chilled serving plate.

About 8 servings

Roquefort-Vegetable Salad

Roquefort-Mayonnaise Dressing:
　3 ounces cream cheese, softened
　3 ounces Roquefort cheese, crumbled
　½ cup light cream
　½ cup mayonnaise
　½ teaspoon Worcestershire sauce
　¼ teaspoon garlic powder
　¼ teaspoon dry mustard
Salad:
　Crisp salad greens
　1 small onion, sliced
　1 cup sliced raw cauliflower
　1 can (16 ounces) cut green beans, chilled and drained
　1 can (13 to 15 ounces) green asparagus spears, chilled and drained
　Snipped parsley

1. For dressing, blend cream cheese with Roquefort cheese.
2. Stir in cream, mayonnaise, Worcestershire sauce, garlic powder, and dry mustard. Beat until fluffy; chill.
3. Half-fill 6 individual salad bowls with the greens. Arrange vegetables on greens.
4. Accompany with a bowl of the dressing garnished with snipped parsley.

6 servings

Zucchini Bread

3 eggs
2 cups sugar
1 cup salad oil
2 cups grated pared zucchini
1 tablespoon vanilla extract
3 cups sifted all-purpose flour
1 teaspoon baking soda
½ teaspoon baking powder
1 teaspoon salt
1 tablespoon cinnamon
½ cup chopped walnuts
½ cup snipped dates

1. Beat eggs well; add sugar, oil, zucchini, and vanilla extract and mix well.
2. Sift flour, baking soda, baking powder, salt, and cinnamon together. Add dry ingredients, nuts, and dates to egg mixture; mix well.
3. Divide batter in 2 greased and floured 9×5×3-inch loaf pans.
4. Bake at 325°F 1 hour.

2 loaves bread

Very Blueberry Pie;
Blueberry Cookie Tarts;
Blueberry Lattice Pie

MIDSUMMER NIGHT SCENE

Crab Meat Mousse

Sweet-Sour Beans in Tomato Shells

Bread Sticks   Butter Curls

Petits Fours (Purchased)

Fruit Compote

Crab Meat Mousse

1½ tablespoons unflavored gelatin
¼ cup cold water
¼ cup lemon juice
1 teaspoon salt
¼ teaspoon paprika
  Few grains pepper
2 cups crab meat, flaked
1 cup whipping cream, whipped

Cucumber Mayonnaise:
1 cup mayonnaise
2 tablespoons lemon juice
1 tablespoon minced parsley
1 medium cucumber, pared and finely chopped

1. Sprinkle gelatin over cold water and lemon juice in a bowl; dissolve over hot water. Mix in salt, paprika, and pepper. Remove from heat and place over ice water about 5 minutes, stirring frequently.
2. Stir in crab meat, then fold in whipped cream. Turn into a 1-quart mold and chill until firm.
3. Unmold onto a chilled plate and serve with Cucumber Mayonnaise.
4. For dressing, blend mayonnaise, lemon juice, and parsley, then mix in cucumber.

About 8 servings

Sweet-Sour Beans in Tomato Shells

⅓ cup cider vinegar
2½ tablespoons dark brown sugar
½ teaspoon salt
1 can (16 ounces) diagonally sliced green beans, drained
1 tablespoon finely chopped onion
6 tomato shells, chilled
1 tablespoon basil, crushed
  Crisp bacon curls

1. Pour a mixture of the vinegar, brown sugar, and salt over the beans and onion in a bowl; toss lightly. Set in refrigerator to marinate 1 hour, tossing occasionally.
2. Sprinkle the inside of each tomato shell with basil and salt. Spoon beans equally into tomato shells. Garnish with bacon curls.

6 servings

SEPTEMBER
Card Parties

September presents a revolving door of activity, with each family member heading off in a different direction. Organizations that lie dormant over the summer spring back to life. Junior is off to Scouts, Sis to Brownies, and Mom and Dad each to individual pursuits.

Some of those adult organizations could be classified Yours, Mine, and Ours. The men have their card night, and the women seek equal time by meeting separately. Then there are mixed couple card nights that bring everyone back together.

Food is an important item of business at these gatherings, and the all-male spread will be quite different from the feminine fare. Of course, when they get together for couples' night, the refreshments should satisfy everybody.

MALE CALL CARD PARTY

The guests may be all male, but chances are that the cooking assignment will fall, at least in part, to the distaff side. The host will welcome help in shopping and stocking the refrigerator with fixings. Come serving time, everything can be put out for help-yourself service.

Cold sandwiches are popular when the chow line forms. An assortment of cold cuts, cheeses, breads, and spreads lets each build his own. Hot sandwiches are appreciated, too, and with careful advance work these can be prepared in short order.

LADIES' NIGHT OUT

There is something about a sandwich loaf that appeals to women, and has an equal but negative charge for men. Take advantage of this all-female gathering to indulge a taste for this specialty.

Ask the bakery to slice a loaf of bread lengthwise, or buy an unsliced loaf and prepare it yourself. A sandwich loaf takes time because its success depends as much on beautiful appearance as it does on flavor. Give yourself an early start when making one.

The fillings (usually three or four in contrasting colors and textures) can be made a day or two ahead. The assembly and decorating of the loaf should be done close to party time, so the bread won't become soggy. Spreading the bread well with butter before adding the fillings helps.

The "frosting" for the sandwich loaf is usually of cream cheese. Sharp process cheese spread can be added for a golden look. Once frosted, your loaf will benefit from decorative touches to the top and sides. Use slices of stuffed olives, cucumbers, radishes, pimento, and hard-cooked eggs to create a design worthy of a caterer.

Depending on the time of your party, a hot sandwich may be more appropriate. If so, either

Mushroom Sauced Sandwiches or Chicken Fiesta Buns would be a good choice.

MIXED COUPLES' CARD PARTY

A mixed couples bridge club offers a good way to get acquainted in a new neighborhood or to be sure of seeing old friends on a regular basis.

When it's your turn to play hostess, consider both masculine and feminine preferences. Your guests will probably want something to munch on and sip while playing.

Strips of carrots, celery, cauliflower, and mushrooms with a low calorie dip are ample. To cut calories from the dip, try our recipe using cottage cheese.

After such sensible snacks, you'll feel justified in splurging on dessert. Make the most of the fresh September fruit coming to market and try your hand at an elegant pie or tarts. Blueberry lovers can hit their stride this month!

MALE CALL CARD PARTY

Roquefort-Tongue Sandwiches

Roquefort Butter
16 slices rye bread
Lettuce
Sliced cooked tongue, ¼ inch thick
⅓ cup butter or margarine

1. Spread Roquefort Butter generously over 8 slices of bread. Place lettuce over each, then sliced tongue.
2. Whip ⅓ cup butter until softened and spread over remaining 8 slices of bread. Complete sandwiches with bread, buttered side down.

8 sandwiches

Note: Sliced cooked turkey may be substituted for the tongue.

Roquefort Butter: Cream **½ cup butter**, **¼ cup crumbled Roquefort cheese**, **2 tablespoons chopped parsley**, **1 tablespoon prepared horseradish**, then blend in **2 teaspoons lemon juice**, a small amount at a time.

Super Sandwich

Curry Butter
French bread slices
Lettuce
Corned beef or roast beef slices
Cheddar cheese slices
Cooked chicken slices
Tomato slices
Crisp bacon slices

1. For each sandwich, spread desired amount of curry butter on 2 slices French bread.
2. Top 1 slice with lettuce and remaining ingredients. Complete sandwich with other bread slice.

Curry Butter: Beat **½ cup butter or margarine** until softened. Blend in **2 teaspoons lemon juice**, a small amount at a time, and then **1 teaspoon curry powder**.

Saucy Beef 'n' Buns

2 tablespoons fat
½ cup chopped onion
1 pound ground beef
1 teaspoon salt
½ teaspoon monosodium glutamate

1. Heat the fat in a large skillet. Add the onion and cook until soft, stirring occasionally. Add the meat and a mixture of salt, monosodium glutamate, and pepper; cook until meat is lightly browned, separating it into pieces with a fork or spoon.

LADIES' NIGHT OUT

Golden Frosted Sandwich Loaf

1 loaf (2-pound) sandwich bread (unsliced)
6 tablespoons butter or margarine, whipped
Creamy Ham Filling
Sliced Tomato Filling
Chicken-Almond Filling
Sharp Cheese Frosting
3 thin tomato slices
Sliced filberts or almonds

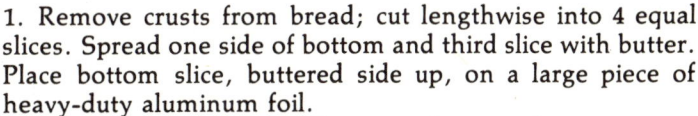

1. Remove crusts from bread; cut lengthwise into 4 equal slices. Spread one side of bottom and third slice with butter. Place bottom slice, buttered side up, on a large piece of heavy-duty aluminum foil.
2. Spread Creamy Ham Filling over bottom slice.
3. Spread second slice of bread with cheese-onion dip mixture; place over ham layer. Top with bacon, then tomato slices and chopped olives. Cover with third slice, buttered side up.
4. Spread Chicken-Almond Filling over third slice of bread and cover with fourth slice. Wrap loaf in the foil and set in refrigerator.
5. About 20 minutes before serving, unwrap loaf and place on a baking sheet. Frost sides and top with Sharp Cheese Frosting. Garnish with tomato slices and nuts.
6. Heat in a 450°F oven 5 minutes, or until lightly browned. Serve at once.

12 to 14 servings

Creamy Ham Filling: Blend thoroughly 1¼ cups ground ham, 3 tablespoons chopped pimento-stuffed olives, 1½ teaspoons finely chopped onion, 5 tablespoons mayonnaise, and 1½ tablespoons prepared horseradish; cover; refrigerate.

Sliced Tomato Filling: Whip 3 ounces cream cheese with ½ package (1 tablespoon) dry onion-dip mix. Cover; set aside. Prepare 3 slices bacon, diced and panbroiled, six ¼-inch tomato slices, and 3 tablespoons chopped ripe olives; cover and refrigerate.

Chicken-Almond Filling: Toss together 1¼ cups chopped cooked chicken, 5 tablespoons chopped salted blanched almonds, 3 tablespoons grated coconut, and 1½ tablespoons capers. Blend ½ cup mayonnaise, 1½ teaspoons red wine vinegar, and ½ teaspoon Italian salad dressing mix. Blend thoroughly with chicken mixture; cover; refrigerate.

Sharp Cheese Frosting: Whip together until fluffy 2 jars (5 ounces each) sharp process cheese spread and 2 packages (3 ounces each) cream cheese. Set aside.

¼ teaspoon black pepper
¾ cup chopped celery
¾ cup chopped green pepper
1 cup chili sauce
1 cup ketchup
Buttered, toasted hamburger buns

2. Blend in celery, green pepper, chili sauce, and ketchup. Simmer, uncovered, about 25 minutes; stir frequently.
3. Serve on buns. Accompany with **corn chips** and **dill pickle strips**.

About 6 servings

Cottage Cheese Dip

1 cup cottage cheese
2 tablespoons mayonnaise-type salad dressing
3 tablespoons minced parsley
2 tablespoons finely chopped onion
2 tablespoons finely chopped chives
1 tablespoon prepared mustard
2 teaspoons crushed mint leaves
2 teaspoons dill seed
1 to 2 teaspoons prepared horseradish
Few drops Tabasco

1. Put the cottage cheese and salad dressing into a bowl. Add any *one* of the remaining ingredients. Beat together until light and fluffy.
2. Accompany with crisp **vegetable sticks or strips, cauliflowerets,** and **radish roses.**

About 1 cup dip

Note: Dip may be served in Green Pepper Shells or Tomato Shells, below.

Green Pepper Shells: Rinse and cut a thin slice from stem end of chilled green peppers. Remove white fiber and seeds.

Tomato Shells: Rinse and chill tomatoes. Cut a slice from tops, remove pulp from tomatoes with a spoon, and invert shells to drain.

Chicken Fiesta Buns

⅓ cup finely chopped green pepper
⅓ cup finely chopped celery
⅓ cup finely chopped onion
1 clove garlic, minced
3 tablespoons butter or margarine
½ cup tomato paste
2 tablespoons Worcestershire sauce
2 tablespoons cider vinegar
1 tablespoon brown sugar
½ teaspoon chili powder
½ teaspoon salt
½ teaspoon monosodium glutamate
¼ teaspoon seasoned pepper
1½ cups chopped cooked chicken or turkey
¼ cup chopped pimento-stuffed olives
8 split frankfurter buns, heated

1. Cook green pepper, celery, onion, and garlic in hot butter about 3 minutes.
2. Stir in a mixture of tomato paste, Worcestershire sauce, vinegar, brown sugar, chili powder, salt, monosodium glutamate, and seasoned pepper; then chicken and olives. Simmer about 10 minutes to blend flavors, stirring occasionally.
3. Spoon mixture into buns; serve immediately.

8 servings

MIXED COUPLES' CARD PARTY

Mushroom-Sauced Sandwiches

- 3 tablespoons butter or margarine
- 2 tablespoons flour
- 1 can (about 10 ounces) condensed cream of mushroom soup
- ¼ cup water
- ½ teaspoon Worcestershire sauce
- 6 slices bread
- 1 tablespoon prepared mustard
- 1 can (12 ounces) chopped ham
- 1 can (14½ ounces) asparagus spears, drained
- Pimento-stuffed olive slices
- Parsley sprigs

1. Melt 2 tablespoons of butter in a saucepan. Blend in flour. Heat until mixture bubbles, stirring constantly. Remove from heat and blend in soup, water, and Worcestershire sauce. Cook until thoroughly heated, stirring constantly.
2. Toast one side only of bread slices. Trim crusts from bread and spread untoasted sides with remaining butter and the mustard. Cut ham into 6 equal slices. Place one ham slice over each bread slice. Arrange 3 asparagus spears on each sandwich. Using a wide spatula, carefully transfer to individual plates.
3. Pour the hot mushroom sauce over each sandwich. Garnish with olive slices and parsley.

6 servings

Very Blueberry Pie

- ½ cup cold water
- ⅓ cup all-purpose flour
- Pinch salt
- 4 cups fresh blueberries, washed and drained
- 1 cup sugar
- ½ cup water
- 1 baked 10-inch pie shell
- Sweetened whipped cream or whipped dessert topping

1. Mix cold water, flour, and salt until smooth.
2. Combine 1 cup of blueberries, sugar, and ½ cup water in a saucepan. Stir and bring to boiling. Add the flour mixture, stirring until mixture thickens. Cool.
3. Mix remaining blueberries into cooled mixture. Turn into pie shell. Chill.
4. To serve, garnish with whipped cream.

One 10-inch pie

Blueberry Lattice-Top Pie

- 1 package pie crust mix
- 4 cups fresh blueberries, washed and drained
- 1 cup sugar
- ¾ cup cold water
- 1 peeled orange, coarsely chopped
- ¼ cup cornstarch

1. Prepare pie crust following package directions. Roll out two-thirds of pie crust; line a 9-inch pie pan. Set aside.
2. Turn blueberries into a saucepan. Add sugar, ½ cup water, and orange; mix. Set over low heat and bring to boiling.
3. Mix cornstarch with remaining ¼ cup water. Stir into boiling mixture. Remove from heat. Cool.
4. Spoon cooled filling into pie crust.
5. Roll out remaining pie crust and cut into strips. Arrange strips in a lattice design over filling. Crimp edge of pie crust.
6. Bake at 400°F 35 to 40 minutes, or until browned. Cool.

One 9-inch pie

Blueberry Cookie Tarts

- 2 tablespoons cornstarch
- ½ cup confectioners' sugar
- ½ cup water
- 2 tablespoons lime juice
- 2 cups fresh blueberries, washed and drained
- 1 cup whipping cream
- 8 (3-inch) tart shells, baked and cooled
- 8 small cookies

1. Mix cornstarch and sugar in a saucepan. Stir in water and lime juice. Add ½ cup blueberries. Cook and stir until mixture comes to boiling; boil 1 minute. Cool.
2. Mix remaining blueberries into cooled mixture.
3. Whip cream and fold in filling. Spoon into tart shells. Top with cookies.

8 tarts

Peach Puffs

- 3 tablespoons butter
- 4 eggs
- 1 cup milk
- Thin outer peel of ½ lemon
- 1 cup sifted all-purpose flour
- 2 tablespoons sugar
- ½ teaspoon salt
- 1½ cups whipping cream
- 3 tablespoons confectioners' sugar
- ¼ teaspoon cinnamon
- ⅛ teaspoon nutmeg
- 4 cups fresh, canned, or thawed frozen peach slices

1. Put 1½ tablespoons butter into each of two 9-inch pie pans. Set in oven while oven is preheating.
2. Put eggs, milk, and lemon peel into an electric blender container. Cover and blend at high speed until thoroughly combined and lemon peel is finely chopped. Add flour, sugar, and salt. Blend at high speed until smooth; scrape down sides of blender container if necessary. Pour half of batter into each pie pan with melted butter.
3. Bake at 400°F 20 to 22 minutes, or until puffed and golden.
4. Whip cream until soft peaks are formed. Beat in confectioners' sugar and spices. Put half of peaches in center of each pancake. Sprinkle with **confectioners' sugar.** Cut into wedges and spoon whipped cream over individual servings.

10 to 12 servings

Filbert Drops

- 1 cup butter
- 1 cup sugar
- 2 eggs
- 1 cup all-purpose flour
- 2½ cups ground filberts (about ½ pound)

1. Cream butter and sugar. Add eggs, one at a time, and beat thoroughly after each addition. Mix in flour and nuts.
2. Chill dough about 2 hours.
3. Using a pastry bag and plain tube, pipe dough onto greased cookie sheets.
4. Bake at 350°F 8 to 10 minutes. Cool cookies on wire racks.

About 7 dozen cookies

OCTOBER Teen Party

Too old for trick-or-treat, but young enough to enjoy the high jinks—that describes the teen-ager on Halloween. He still enjoys putting on a costume, so to avoid that "all dressed up and nowhere to go" feeling, let him have a party at home.

Teens are happiest at do-it-yourself parties. Having something to do is a good ice-breaker for them and a great worksaver for Mom. Not that it should be parent's night out; adults should stand by to help when needed.

So if the high schooler in your family votes for an October party, put him or her to work getting out the invitations and making all the preparations.

ACTIVITIES

Teen age is an active age. Guests will want to do more at the party than merely eat, so have your young host or hostess think of ways to keep everyone busy. Records and dancing will probably take top priority, but this bunch isn't too sophisticated for a few games and other activities.

Halloween itself suggests a few: carving pumpkins, bobbing for apples (preferably on the patio to avoid spills inside), or a ghost walk if your teenager is willing to set one up.

Artsy-craftsy parties are fun for teen-agers at any time of the year and work well with adult supervision. Invite everyone to bring a T-shirt or some other inexpensive bit of clothing, and do a little tie-dying in the backyard or basement. Two or three pans of various dyes plus heavy string for tying are the only supplies needed.

Potato carving is fun, too. To make printing pads, fold paper towels in foil pans, then pour a generous amount of tempera paint into each pan. Let the guests stamp their carved potato halves on newsprint, paper towels, or tissue. Varying the texture of the background paper makes the prints more interesting.

Mobiles can be made from coat hangers. Provide string and a variety of baubles, and let the young artists use their imagination.

Long strips of wrapping paper attached to the basement wall, a supply of paint, and big brushes will result in a mural that can be completed during the course of the party.

Prepare the party room or yard for whatever activity you plan so cleanup will be easy and accidents no cause for alarm.

THE FOOD

When it's time for eats, let everyone get into the act. Choose food they can help assemble such as make-your-own pizzas or tacos. Or if you're not serving a whole meal, let 'em eat cake—one they've stirred up themselves from a mix.

74 OCTOBER—TEEN PARTY

Bear in mind though, that even guest-participation refreshments require some advance work. Lining things up, washing, peeling, and measuring are best done ahead of time. Even for a project as simple as popcorn balls, have oil in the pan, the corn measured, and all the ingredients for the syrup waiting in the saucepan. The guests can do the fun part—popping the corn, making the syrup, and getting it all together into balls.

For something more ambitious, such as make-your-own pizzas, have everything lined up cafeteria-style. Then let the guests file through the kitchen to concoct their pizzas, with the suggestion that they arrange ingredients in a design so they'll recognize their own pizzas after baking.

Pizza naturally goes with an Italian salad. For this, greens can be torn and chilled, ready to top at the last minute with a bottled Italian dressing.

Since tacos are assembled just before eating, you or the young host or hostess could prepare the fillers in advance, keeping meat and sauce hot until serving time. Then let everyone line up and fill his taco as he pleases.

Desserts for teens needn't be fancy but they should be ample. Calories are rarely a worry since high schoolers grow fast and move at a pace to burn off lots of energy. Brownies, chocolate chip cookies, and cakes are big winners.

So is candy, and cooks will probably enjoy making their own. The taffy pull is a real old-timer as party ideas go. Make the candy ahead of time so it will be just right for pulling when the guests are ready.

RECIPES FOR A TEEN PARTY

Snack Mix

6 cups popped corn
4 cups pretzel rings
1 can (4 ounces) shoestring potatoes
¼ cup butter or margarine, melted
1 tablespoon onion soup mix

1. Combine popcorn, pretzel rings, and shoestring potatoes in a 13×9-inch baking pan.
2. Combine butter and onion soup mix; pour over popcorn mixture, stirring to coat evenly.
3. Heat in a 325°F oven 10 minutes, stirring once.

About 12 cups

Taco Dogs

12 skinless frankfurters
12 taco shells
1 can (2 ounces) taco sauce
1½ cups shredded lettuce
1½ cups shredded Cheddar cheese
1½ cups chopped tomato

To assemble taco dogs, place frankfurters in taco shells; top with taco sauce, shredded lettuce, cheese, and chopped tomato.

12 Taco Dogs

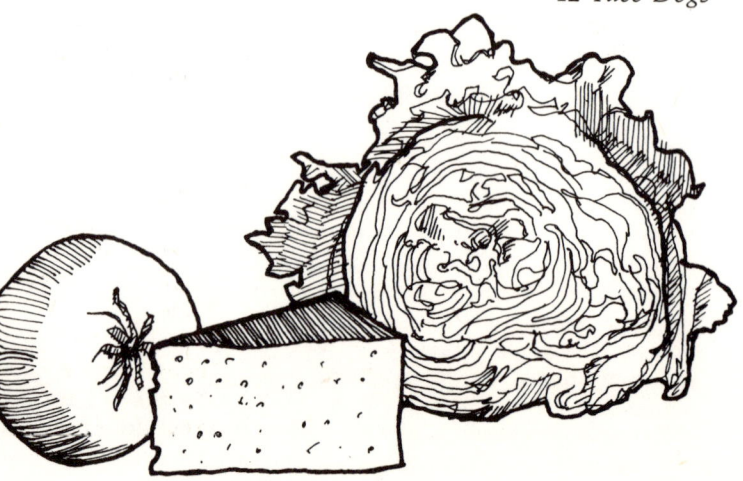

Chili Dogs

- 1 pound ground beef
- 1 tablespoon chili seasoning mix
- 1 can (15 ounces) tomato sauce with tomato bits
- Water
- 12 skinless frankfurters
- 12 frankfurter buns

1. Brown ground beef in a skillet; drain. Add seasoning mix and tomato sauce; simmer until flavors are blended.
2. Meanwhile, bring water to boiling in a large saucepan. Add frankfurters, cover, remove from heat, and let stand 7 minutes.
3. Place frankfurters in buns; top with chili mixture.

12 Chili Dogs

Salami Pizza Loaf

- 2 packages (9 ounces each) refrigerated roll dough for crescents
- ¼ cup canned pizza sauce
- 8 slices salami
- 1 package (4 ounces) shredded mozzarella cheese
- 1 egg, beaten
- 1 tablespoon sesame seed

1. Remove dough from 1 package crescent rolls; unroll carefully and pinch seams together to seal; place on greased cookie sheet.
2. Spread dough with pizza sauce; arrange salami slices on top and sprinkle with cheese.
3. Remove dough from remaining package of crescent rolls; pinch seams together to seal. Cut into 3 lengthwise strips; place one strip along each side of loaf, pressing to seal. Cut remaining strip into thirds lengthwise; braid. Place along center of loaf, pressing ends to seal. Brush with beaten egg; sprinkle with sesame seed.
4. Bake at 375°F 15 to 20 minutes, or until golden brown. Cut in crosswise strips to serve.

8 servings

Brown Sugar Taffy

- 2¼ cups firmly packed dark brown sugar
- 1½ cups light corn syrup
- 4 teaspoons cider vinegar
- ¼ teaspoon salt
- ½ cup undiluted evaporated milk
- Butter

1. Combine the brown sugar, corn syrup, vinegar, and salt in a heavy 3-quart saucepan. Set over low heat and stir until sugar is dissolved. Increase heat and bring to boiling, stirring constantly.
2. Add evaporated milk slowly, stirring constantly, so that boiling does not stop. Set candy thermometer in place. Cook, stirring constantly, until mixture reaches 248°F (firm-ball stage). During cooking, wash down crystals from sides of pan with a pastry brush dipped in water.
3. Remove from heat and remove thermometer. Immediately pour mixture into a buttered shallow pan or platter; do not scrape saucepan.
4. When mixture is just cool enough to handle, pull a small portion at a time with buttered hands. Work in a cool place. Pull until candy is ivory colored and no longer sticky to the touch.
5. Twist pulled strip slightly and place on waxed paper or a board. Cut with scissors or sharp knife into 1-inch pieces.
6. For storing, wrap pieces in moisture-vaporproof material and store in a tightly covered container in a cool, dry place.

About 2 pounds

Jack-O-Lantern Cake

- 1 package (about 19 ounces) lemon or orange chiffon cake mix
- 2 eggs
- Lemon-lime carbonated beverage
- ⅔ cup canned pumpkin
- 1 teaspoon pumpkin pie spice
- Frosting
- ⅓ of a firm banana, peeled

1. Prepare cake following package directions, using carbonated beverage for the liquid in both portions of the mix. Add pumpkin and spice to batter portion of the mix. Combine as directed.
2. Turn batter into 2 ungreased 2½-quart ovenproof mixing bowls.
3. Bake at 300°F about 1 hour, or until cake tests done.
4. Immediately invert bowls on wire racks to cool cakes. Running a spatula around inside of bowls, loosen cooled cakes and carefully remove from bowls.
5. Prepare and tint the Frosting.
6. To frost, place one cake on serving plate, rounded side down. Spread top surface generously with frosting and cover with second cake, rounded side up, forming a pumpkin shape. Frost the entire outside surface of cake, using long vertical strokes to resemble a pumpkin. Cover the piece of banana with green-tinted frosting and place it, cut side down, on top center of cake.
7. Make a face on the pumpkin using **gumdrops, licorice,** and **candy corn** for the eyes, nose, mouth, and teeth.

About 16 servings

Frosting: Following package directions, prepare **2 packages fluffy frosting mix** using **lemon-lime carbonated beverage** for the hot liquid. Tint ¼ cup of the frosting green to use for the "stem" of the pumpkin. Tint remaining frosting orange, using about **1¼ teaspoons yellow food coloring** and **¼ teaspoon red food coloring.**

Special Blender Cheese Dip

- ¼ pound blue cheese, crumbled
- 1 package (3 ounces) cream cheese
- ¼ cup dairy sour cream
- 2 tablespoons pineapple juice
- 2 teaspoons Worcestershire sauce
- ½ teaspoon monosodium glutamate
- 1 drop Tabasco
- 4 or 5 sprigs parsley
- 1 slice onion

1. Put all ingredients into an electric blender container.
2. Cover and turn on motor. Blend until smooth.

About 1½ cups dip

OCTOBER—TEEN PARTY 77

Caramel Popcorn or Balls

- 5 quarts popped corn
- 2 cups firmly packed brown sugar
- ½ cup light corn syrup
- 1 cup margarine
- Pinch cream of tartar
- 1 teaspoon baking soda

1. Set popped corn in a 200°F oven.
2. Combine brown sugar, corn syrup, margarine, and cream of tartar in a large heavy saucepan. Bring to boiling, stirring until sugar is dissolved. If using a candy thermometer, set in place. Boil rapidly about 5 minutes (300°F).
3. Remove from heat; add baking soda and stir well. Pour syrup over warm popped corn.
4. If making balls, shape with buttered hands.
5. If making Caramel Popcorn, put into oven and stir every 15 minutes for 1 hour.
6. Take the caramel corn from the oven and turn out onto paper. Cool.

Mallow-Nut Brownies

Brownies:
- ½ cup butter
- 1½ ounces (1½ squares) unsweetened chocolate
- 2 eggs
- 1 cup sugar
- ¾ cup all-purpose flour
- ½ teaspoon baking powder
- ⅛ teaspoon salt
- ¾ cup pecans, coarsely chopped

Topping:
- 1 package (12 ounces) semisweet chocolate pieces
- 2 tablespoons butter
- 12 marshmallows, cut in quarters (or use 1⅓ cups miniature marshmallows)
- ½ cup coarsely chopped salted pecans

1. For brownies, melt butter and chocolate together; set aside to cool.
2. Beat eggs and sugar until thick and piled softly; add cooled chocolate mixture and beat until blended.
3. Mix flour, baking powder, and salt together; add in halves to chocolate mixture, mixing until blended after each addition. Stir in pecans.
4. Turn batter into a greased 9×9×2-inch baking pan and spread evenly.
5. Bake at 350°F 35 to 40 minutes.
6. Meanwhile, for topping, melt chocolate pieces and butter. Stir in marshmallows and pecans into melted chocolate.
7. Immediately spread marshmallow-nut mixture over the baked brownies; cool. Cut into squares.

3 dozen cookies

Blonde Brownies

- ¼ cup butter or margarine
- 1 cup firmly packed brown sugar
- 1 egg
- ½ teaspoon vanilla extract
- ¾ cup all-purpose flour
- 1 teaspoon baking powder
- ½ teaspoon salt
- ¾ cup walnuts, chopped

1. Melt butter in a saucepan over low heat. Remove from heat and blend in brown sugar. Set aside to cool.
2. Add egg and vanilla extract to brown sugar mixture and stir well.
3. Mix flour, baking powder, and salt; blend with mixture in saucepan. Stir in nuts.
4. Turn into a greased 8-inch square pan; spread evenly.
5. Bake at 350°F 25 minutes; do not overbake.
6. While still warm, cut into squares or bars.

About 1½ dozen cookies

Pumpkin Jumbos

- 2 cups dark seedless raisins
- 1½ cups water
- 4½ cups sifted all-purpose flour
- 1 teaspoon baking powder
- 1 teaspoon baking soda
- 1 teaspoon salt
- 1¼ cups butter or margarine
- 1 teaspoon cinnamon
- ¼ teaspoon allspice
- ¼ teaspoon nutmeg
- 1 teaspoon vanilla extract
- 2 cups sugar
- 3 eggs
- 1 cup chopped walnuts

Creamy Orange Frosting:
- ¼ cup butter or margarine
- 1½ teaspoons vanilla extract
- ⅛ teaspoon salt
- 1 pound (about 3¼ cups) confectioners' sugar
- 1 egg yolk
- 2 to 3 tablespoons orange juice
- Red and yellow food coloring

1. Combine raisins and water in a saucepan. Bring to boiling and simmer 5 minutes. Drain, reserving ½ cup liquid. Set raisins and liquid aside.
2. Sift flour, baking powder, baking soda, and salt together; set aside.
3. Cream butter with spices and vanilla extract; add sugar gradually, beating until fluffy. Add eggs, one at a time, beating thoroughly after each addition.
4. Add dry ingredients alternately with raisin liquid, mixing until blended after each addition. Mix in raisins and walnuts.
5. Drop by heaping tablespoonfuls 2 inches apart onto lightly greased cookie sheets.
6. Bake at 400°F about 10 minutes.
7. Remove to wire racks. When cool, frost with Creamy Orange Frosting.
8. For frosting, cream the butter with vanilla extract and salt. Add the confectioners' sugar gradually, creaming until blended. Add egg yolk and beat until smooth.
9. Add the orange juice gradually, beating until frosting is of desired consistency. Blend in food coloring, one drop at a time (approximately 3 drops of red and 6 drops of yellow), until frosting is tinted a light orange.
10. Decorate to resemble jack-o'-lantern faces. With a wooden pick or fine brush dipped in **melted chocolate,** draw lines to indicate grooves in pumpkin and to make the face. Use a piece of **citron or angelica** for stem.

About 4 dozen cookies

NOVEMBER
Melting Potluck

Turkey with trimmings—that's menu shorthand for the traditional Thanksgiving dinner. And who's to improve upon tradition? For this special day, give your family the dinner they're anticipating. Of such meals, memories are made.

Slight variations on the customary dishes are acceptable, even welcome in some cases. Follow our suggestions for a few innovations in the family favorites.

November lends itself to parties that vary the Thanksgiving theme. This holiday is meant to honor our forefathers. For most Americans, the ancestral home was a country other than the United States. And most of us enjoy the opportunity to wave those banners occasionally.

So in November give the essence of the melting pot to the potluck party. Invite friends to "come as your ancestor" and bring a dish reminiscent of the former fatherland.

Much of the world's population dresses according to Western standards today, so your invitation could suggest that guests dress as their ancestors did two or three centuries ago. For the English who might wonder what to wear, suggest a Pilgrim's starched collar and tall hat or bonnet.

Some people are reluctant to dress for costume parties. Encourage them by offering a prize for any of a number of categories: the costume representing the most distant land, the smallest country, the biggest country, and so on. Try, if possible, to have a small prize for everyone. The point of the awards should be to let everyone share the spotlight rather than to pick the costume that is best.

PLANNING THE FOOD

"Taking potluck" used to mean "anything goes." Each cook brought whatever he pleased. Today the hostess usually prefers to make assignments either of category or specific dish so the menu will provide all the essentials. But since the point of the Melting Potluck is to let guests share their heritage, it would be more in keeping to assign categories only and let guests bring an heirloom recipe of their own choosing.

While you might limit a sit-down dinner party to six or eight, a potluck dinner—especially in costume—is more fun with a crowd. Perhaps by setting up card tables or providing trays for lap service you can stretch the number to twelve, five couples plus the host couple.

One plan for dividing the menu for this number is to provide the cocktails, meat dish, bread, and beverage yourself. Ask guests to bring a dish to serve twelve in each of the following categories: appetizers, pasta, vegetable casserole, salad, and dessert. Within this framework there is plenty of leeway to exercise imagination and find representative foreign dishes.

80 NOVEMBER—MELTING POTLUCK

PLANNING DECORATIONS

A basketwork cornucopia spilling out the multi-colored fruits of the fall harvest is a popular Thanksgiving season centerpiece. Lacking a cornucopia, a basket or bowl filled with fruits or vegetables in contrasting colors and shapes will serve your purpose. To accent the melting pot theme, surround the centerpiece with miniature flags of other lands, arranged fan style from the base of the basket.

GIVING THE PARTY

On party day anticipate the needs of your guests for refrigerator, oven, and counter space. The salad and dessert will probably need temporary refrigeration, and some of the other dishes will need to bake or stay warm during the hospitality hour. Be prepared for those inevitable requests for serving pieces.

If you don't have table service for twelve, provide attractive paper plates and cups in harvest hues. Paper napkins will do, but if there is time make cloth napkins from inexpensive fabric. A table runner from the same fabric will complete a handsome table setting.

The recipes that follow are those for a traditional Thanksgiving dinner and for foreign dishes that might find their way to a Melting Potluck.

TRADITIONAL THANKSGIVING DINNER

Thanksgiving Wine Bowl

Roast Turkey

Candied Cranberries

Candied Sweet Potatoes

Buttered Green Beans

Pecan-Topped Pumpkin Pie

Coffee   Milk

Thanksgiving Wine Bowl

2 cups apple cider or apple juice
½ cup sugar
2 sticks cinnamon
2 dozen whole cloves
2 quarts dry white wine

1. Combine cider and sugar in a large porcelain saucepan.
2. In bag made of cheesecloth, tie together cinnamon and cloves. Add to ingredients in saucepan and boil 5 minutes.
3. Remove spices from cider. Add wine. Cook only until mixture is thoroughly warm; do not boil.
4. Serve in heatproof punch bowl and ladle into heatproof punch cups with more cinnamon sticks for stirrers, if desired.

16 to 20 servings

TOP: Salami Pizza Loaf; Chili Dogs; Taco Dogs
BOTTOM: Brownie Fruitcake; Irish Fruitcake;
Banana-Walnut Fruitcake; White Walnut Fruitcake;
Double Walnut Fruitcake

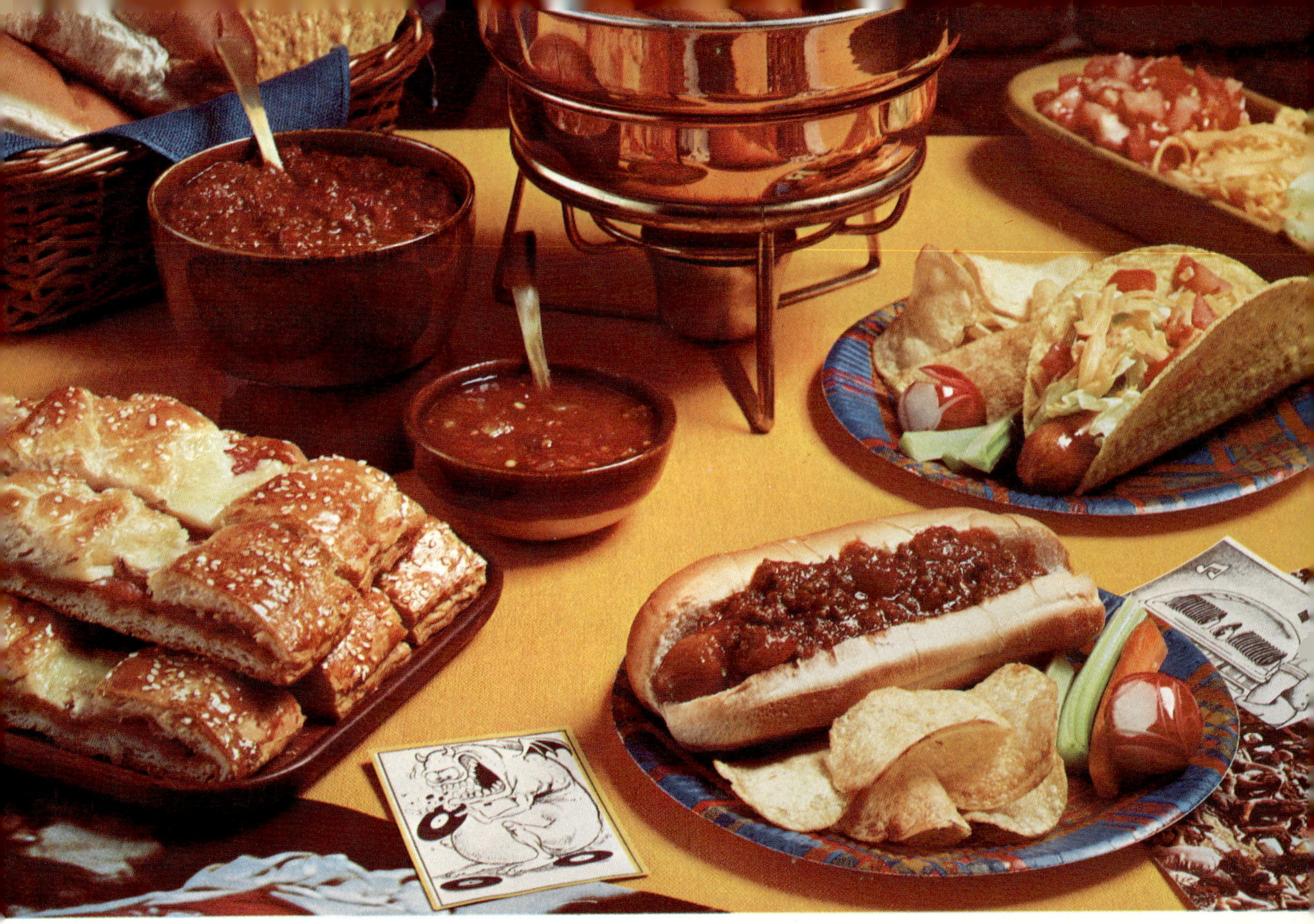

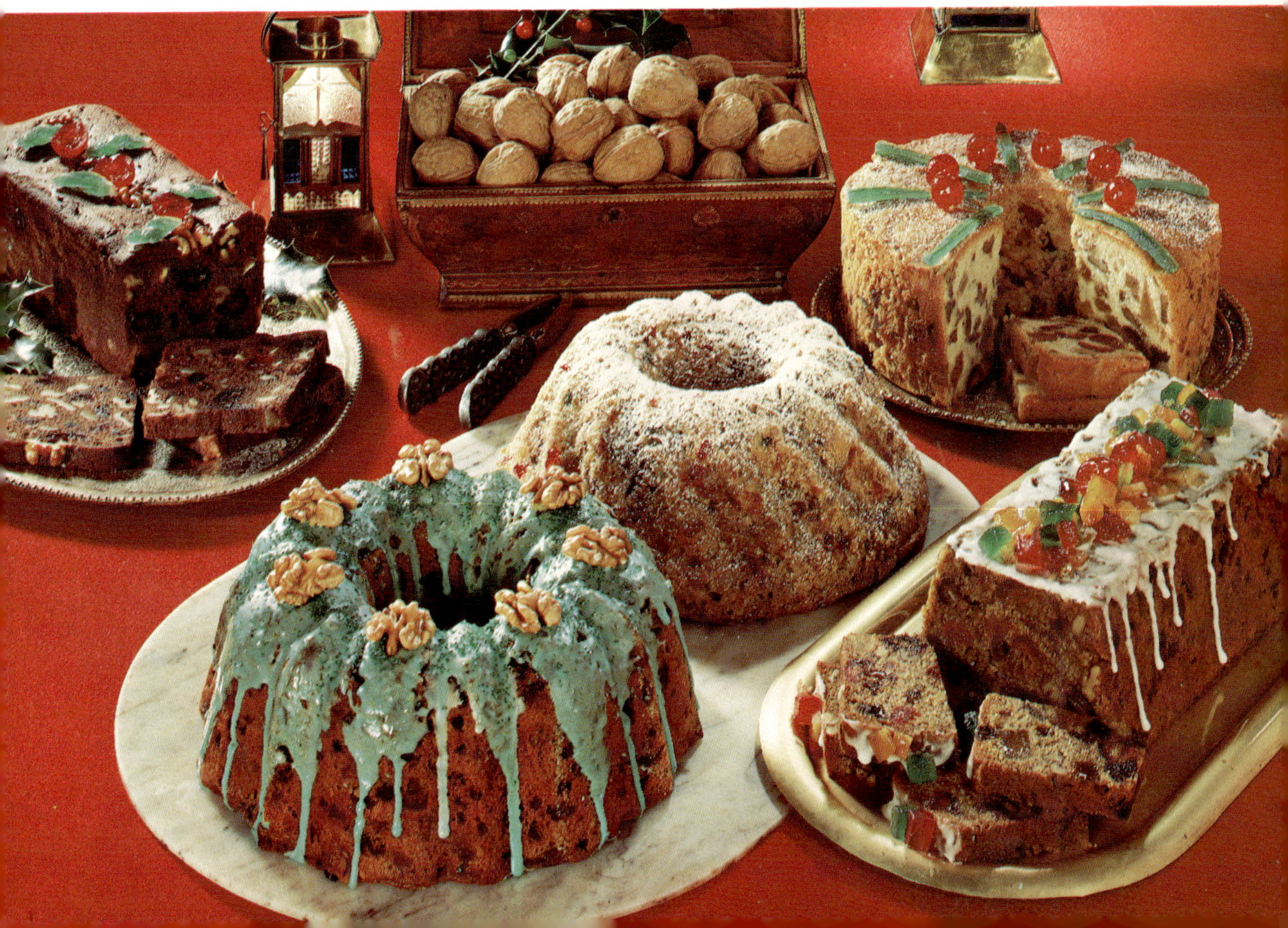

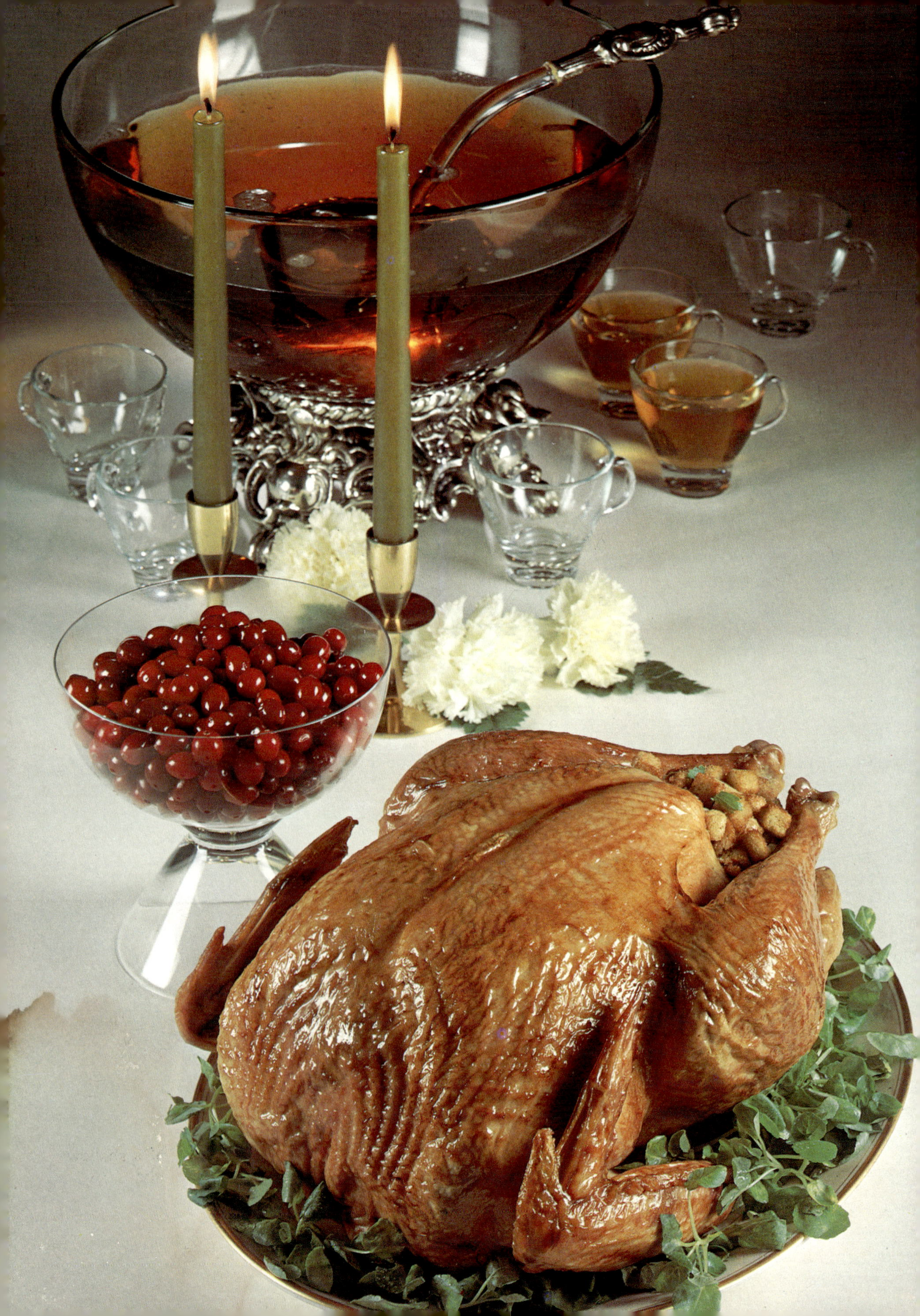

Roast Turkey

1 ready-to-cook turkey (10 to 12 pounds)
Cooked Giblets and Broth
Stuffing (favorite recipe or a mix)
Salt
Melted fat
Gravy (favorite recipe)

1. If desired, cook giblets and broth for stuffing and gravy.
2. Rinse bird with cold water. Drain and pat dry with absorbent paper or soft cloth.
3. Prepare stuffing, adding chopped giblets, if using.
4. Rub body and neck cavities with salt. Fill lightly with stuffing. (Extra stuffing may be put into a greased covered baking dish or wrapped in aluminum foil and baked with turkey the last hour of roasting time.)
5. Fasten neck skin to back with skewer and bring wing tips onto back. Push drumsticks under band of skin at tail, or tie with cord. Set, breast up, on rack in shallow roasting pan. Brush with melted fat.
6. If meat thermometer is used, insert it in center of inside thigh muscle or thickest part of breast meat. Be sure that tip does not touch bone. If desired, cover top and sides of turkey with cheesecloth moistened with melted fat. Keep cloth moist during roasting by brushing occasionally with fat from the bottom of pan.
7. Roast, uncovered, at 325°F 4 to 4½ hours. When turkey is two-thirds done, cut band of skin or cord at drumsticks. Continue roasting until turkey tests done (the thickest part of the drumstick feels soft when pressed with fingers and meat thermometer registers 180° to 185°F).
8. For easier carving, let turkey stand 20 to 30 minutes, keeping it warm. Meanwhile, prepare gravy from drippings; use broth and chopped giblets if available.
9. Remove cord and skewers from turkey and place on heated platter. Garnish platter as desired.

About 16 servings

Note: If desired, turkey may be roasted in heavy-duty aluminum foil. Brush bird thoroughly with melted fat; wrap securely in foil; close with a drugstore or lock fold to prevent leakage of drippings. Place, breast up, in roasting pan (omit rack). Roast a 10- to 12-pound turkey at 450°F about 3 hours. About 20 minutes before end of roasting time, remove from oven. Quickly unfold foil to edge of pan. Insert meat thermometer. Return uncovered bird to oven and complete cooking. (Turkey will brown sufficiently in this time.)

Cooked Giblets and Broth: Put **turkey neck and giblets** (except liver) into a saucepan with **1 large onion, sliced, parsley, celery with leaves, 1 medium-sized bay leaf, 2 teaspoons salt,** and **1 quart water.** Cover and simmer until giblets are tender, about 2 hours; add the liver the last 15 minutes of cooking. Strain; reserve broth for gravy. Chop the giblets; reserve for stuffing and gravy.

Candied Cranberries

2 cups fresh cranberries
1 cup sugar

1. Wash cranberries and spread over bottom of a shallow baking dish. Sprinkle with sugar and cover tightly.
2. Bake at 350°F 1 hour, stirring occasionally.
3. Chill before serving.

Thanksgiving Wine Bowl;
Candied Cranberries;
Roast Turkey

MELTING POTLUCK DINNER PARTY

APPETIZERS
Angels on Horseback (England)

Empanadas (Chile)

MEAT DISHES
Veal Steak Cordon Bleu (Switzerland)

Carbonada Criolla (Argentina)

PASTA
Fettucine al Burro Alfredo (Italy)

Mexican Rice

VEGETABLE DISHES
Ratatouille (France)

Hungarian Creamed Spinach

SALAD
Hot Potato Salad (Germany)

Polish Tomato Salad

DESSERT
Farmer's Sunday Cake (Ireland)

Applecake with Vanilla Sauce (Sweden)

Angels on Horseback (England)

12 to 16 medium oysters
Freshly ground pepper
12 to 16 thin slices bacon
1 lemon, thinly sliced
Parsley sprigs

1. Open oysters. (Use only tightly closed oysters; discard the half-opened ones.) Season shucked oysters with pepper and wrap a slice of bacon around each; secure with a wooden pick or skewer.
2. Arrange on rack of a broiler pan. Place pan under broiler so tops of appetizers are about 4 inches from heat. Broil 7 to 8 minutes, turning several times to brown bacon evenly.
3. Arrange appetizers on a serving plate with lemon half-slices. Garnish with parsley.

12 to 16 appetizers

Empanadas (Chile)

Dough:
- 4½ cups all-purpose flour
- ½ teaspoon baking powder
- ½ teaspoon salt
- 1 cup butter, chilled
- 2 eggs, slightly beaten
- ½ cup lukewarm milk

Filling:
- 2 to 3 tablespoons oil
- ½ pound ground pork (or half beef)
- 1 large clove garlic, crushed
- ½ cup finely chopped onion
- ⅓ cup finely chopped celery
- 2 large ripe tomatoes, peeled and chopped
- ⅓ cup raisins, chopped
- 8 pimento-stuffed olives, finely chopped
- ½ teaspoon salt
- 1 teaspoon sugar
- ¼ teaspoon marjoram leaves
- ¼ teaspoon paprika
- 1 canned small hot chili, minced; or ½ teaspoon chopped dried chili
- 2 hard-cooked eggs, finely chopped
- Egg white, slightly beaten
- Shortening, heated to 365° to 375°F

1. For dough, mix flour with baking powder and salt in a mixing bowl; cut in half of the butter, using a pastry blender or two knives. Add a mixture of eggs and milk; mix only until dough can be formed into a ball.
2. Turn onto a lightly floured pastry canvas and roll into a rectangle. Cut remaining chilled fat into small pieces and distribute over surface of dough. Fold dough over several times; knead gently until very smooth and easy to handle, using as little flour on canvas as necessary. Form into a ball. Wrap well and chill several hours or overnight.
3. To prepare filling, heat oil in a skillet; add meat, garlic, onion, and celery; cook and stir about 5 minutes, or until meat is browned. Add tomato and cook 3 minutes. Mix in raisins, olives, seasonings, and eggs.
4. Roll out dough, a half at a time, until very thin; cut into 4-inch rounds. Spoon 1 heaped tablespoon of filling on each; brush edges with egg white and press to seal.
5. Deep-fry empanadas in hot fat until golden brown on both sides.

About 4 dozen empanadas

Veal Steak Cordon Bleu (Switzerland)

- 8 veal cutlets
- Salt and pepper
- Ketchup
- 4 thin slices cooked ham
- 4 slices Swiss cheese
- Flour
- 1 egg, beaten
- Bread crumbs
- Shortening
- Lemon wedges (optional)

1. Flatten meat by pounding on both sides with a meat hammer. Season with salt and pepper. Spread a thin layer of ketchup over one side of each steak. Fold a slice of ham over a slice of cheese and put between two veal steaks (ketchup side inside). Secure with wooden picks.
2. Coat steaks with flour, then beaten egg, and finally bread crumbs.
3. Heat a small amount of shortening in a heavy skillet, add steaks, and cook until evenly browned on both sides and meat is tender.
4. Serve with lemon wedges, if desired.

4 servings

Note: If thicker veal steaks are used, cut a pocket lengthwise in steak and insert ham and cheese.

Carbonada Criolla (Argentina)

- 2 pounds veal, cut in pieces
- ½ cup all-purpose flour
- 1 teaspoon salt
- Lard for frying
- 2 cloves garlic, crushed
- 2 medium onions, chopped
- 2 green peppers, cut in strips
- 3 medium tomatoes, cut in wedges
- Soup greens
- 1 cup chopped celery; or use celery root (celeriac)
- ¼ cup chopped parsley
- 1½ teaspoons salt
- ½ teaspoon thyme
- ¼ to ½ teaspoon cayenne pepper
- ¼ teaspoon marjoram
- 6 peppercorns
- 1 bay leaf
- 1 cup white wine, such as sauterne
- 1 cup beef broth or bouillon
- 4 potatoes, pared and cubed
- ½ pound pumpkin meat, cubed
- 2 apples, pared and cut in wedges
- 1 small can (about 8 ounces) whole kernel corn, drained
- 2 peaches, peeled and cut in wedges
- ½ pound grapes
- Fluffy hot rice

1. Coat veal with a mixture of flour and 1 teaspoon salt.
2. Heat a small amount of lard in a large saucepot, add meat, and brown well on all sides.
3. Heat a small amount of lard in a skillet. Add garlic, onion, green pepper, and tomato; cook until lightly browned. Turn into saucepot with meat. Add soup greens (see Note), celery, seasonings, wine, and broth; mix well. Cover and simmer about 1 hour. Add potato, pumpkin, and apple; cook 15 minutes. Add corn, peaches, and grapes; mix. Heat to serving temperature.
4. Serve in a hollowed-out pumpkin half. Accompany with rice.

About 10 servings

Note: For soup greens, buy prepackaged or use all or a choice of the following vegetables (carrot, celery, leek, onion, parsnip, turnip) and herbs (parsley, tarragon, thyme).

Fettuccine al Burro Alfredo (Italy)

- 1 pound egg noodles
- Salt
- Unsalted butter
- Parmesan or Romano cheese, finely grated

1. Cook noodles in boiling salted water until barely tender (*al dente*); drain thoroughly.
2. Bring quickly to the table in a heated serving bowl and rapidly toss and twirl with a generous amount of fresh unsalted butter and cheese so that the butter and cheese melt so quickly that the fettuccine can be served piping hot.

About 8 servings

Mexican Rice

- ¼ cup finely chopped onion
- 1 small clove garlic, minced
- 1 cup uncooked rice
- 3 tablespoons cooking or salad oil
- ½ teaspoon chili powder
- 1 teaspoon salt
- 2½ cups water

1. Add onion, garlic, and rice to hot oil in a heavy saucepan; fry about 3 minutes, or until golden, stirring occasionally.
2. Stir in a mixture of chili powder and salt. Add water, stir, and cover tightly. Bring to boiling and simmer until rice is tender, about 25 minutes.

About 8 servings

NOVEMBER—MELTING POTLUCK 85

Ratatouille (France)

- 1 medium eggplant, pared and cut in 3×½-inch slices
- 2 zucchini, cut in ¼-inch slices
- 1 teaspoon salt
- ½ cup olive oil
- 2 onions, thinly sliced
- 2 green peppers, thinly sliced
- 2 cloves garlic, minced
- 3 tomatoes, peeled and cut in strips
- 1 cup sliced pimento-stuffed olives
- ¼ cup chopped parsley
- 1 teaspoon salt
- ¼ teaspoon pepper

1. Toss eggplant and zucchini with 1 teaspoon salt and let stand 30 minutes. Drain and then dry on absorbent paper.
2. Heat ¼ cup of the oil in a large skillet and lightly brown eggplant strips and zucchini slices. Remove with slotted spoon and set aside.
3. Heat remaining ¼ cup oil in the skillet; cook onion and green pepper until tender. Stir in garlic. Put tomato strips on top; cover and cook 5 minutes. Gently stir in eggplant, zucchini, olives, parsley, 1 teaspoon salt, and the pepper.
4. Simmer, covered, 20 minutes. Uncover and cook 5 minutes; baste with juices from bottom of pan. Serve hot or cold.

6 to 8 servings

Hungarian Creamed Spinach

- 2 packages (10 ounces each) frozen chopped spinach
- ¼ cup butter or margarine
- ¼ cup all-purpose flour
- ½ teaspoon salt
- ¼ teaspoon garlic salt
- ¼ teaspoon pepper
- 1½ cups cream
- 2 eggs, slightly beaten

1. Cook spinach following package directions.
2. Meanwhile, heat butter in a saucepan. Blend in the flour and seasonings. Heat until bubbly. Gradually add the cream, stirring until smooth. Bring to boiling; continue to stir and cook 1 to 2 minutes. Remove from heat. Vigorously stir a small amount of sauce into the beaten eggs. Immediately blend into hot sauce, stirring until smooth.
3. Drain spinach thoroughly and mix into the hot sauce.

About 6 servings

Hot Potato Salad (Germany)

- 12 slices bacon, diced and fried until crisp (reserve 6 tablespoons drippings)
- 3 medium onions, chopped (2 cups)
- 1 cup less 2 tablespoons cider vinegar
- 1½ tablespoons sugar
- 1½ teaspoons salt
- ¾ teaspoon monosodium glutamate
- ¼ teaspoon pepper
- 2 to 3 pounds potatoes, cooked, peeled, and cut in ¼-inch slices

1. Heat bacon drippings in a skillet. Add onion and cook until tender, stirring occasionally. Stir in vinegar, sugar, salt, monosodium glutamate, and pepper; heat to boiling. Mix in bacon.
2. Pour over potato slices in a serving dish and toss lightly to coat evenly. Garnish with **snipped parsley** and **paprika.** Serve hot.

About 6 servings

Polish Tomato Salad

- ½ cup finely chopped onion, about 1 medium
- 1 teaspoon salt
- 5 hard-cooked eggs, chopped
- 1 pint dairy sour cream
- 7 tomatoes

1. Early in the day sprinkle onion with salt and toss to coat evenly. Mix chopped hard-cooked eggs with onion. Cover and refrigerate.
2. At serving time, add sour cream to eggs and onion for dressing. Slice tomatoes and arrange on serving platter, overlapping edges. Salt tomatoes and top with dressing.

10 servings

Farmer's Sunday Cake (Ireland)

2½ cups sifted cake flour
1¼ teaspoons baking soda
¾ cup butter or margarine
1 teaspoon vanilla extract
1 tablespoon grated lemon peel
¾ cup sugar
2 eggs, well beaten
1 cup buttermilk
1 cup golden raisins
¼ cup diced assorted candied fruits
⅓ cup (about 15) chopped green maraschino cherries, drained

Lemon Butter Frosting:
¼ cup butter or margarine
1 teaspoon vanilla extract
1 teaspoon grated lemon peel
2 cups sifted confectioners' sugar
1 tablespoon lemon juice

1. Grease bottoms only of two 8-inch round layer cake pans; line with waxed paper cut to fit bottoms; grease waxed paper.
2. Sift flour and baking soda together.
3. Cream butter, vanilla extract, and lemon peel together until butter is softened. Add sugar gradually, creaming until fluffy after each addition. Add beaten eggs in thirds to creamed mixture, beating well after each addition.
4. Beating only until smooth after each addition, alternately add dry ingredients in fourths and buttermilk in thirds to the creamed mixture. Finally, beat only until smooth.
5. Mix fruit and blend mixture into batter. Turn batter into prepared cake pans.
6. Bake at 350°F 30 to 35 minutes, or until a cake tester or wooden pick comes out clean when inserted in center of cake. Invert onto wire rack; remove waxed paper, and turn cake, right side up. Cool completely.
7. For lemon butter frosting, cream butter, vanilla extract, and lemon peel until butter is softened. Add confectioners' sugar gradually, beating well after each addition. Add lemon juice and beat until of spreading consistency.
8. When cake is cooled, fill and frost cake with frosting. If desired, decorate with green cherries.

One 8-inch round layer cake

Applecake with Vanilla Sauce (Sweden)

13 rusks (4 ounces), finely crushed (about 2 cups crumbs)
¼ cup sugar
⅓ cup butter or margarine, melted
2½ cups thick applesauce
¼ cup butter or margarine
¼ cup confectioners' sugar

Vanilla Sauce:
⅓ cup butter or margarine, softened
½ cup sugar
6 egg yolks
¾ cup boiling water
1 teaspoon vanilla extract

1. Blend the crumbs and sugar in a bowl. Toss lightly with the melted butter until crumbs are evenly coated.
2. Generously grease a 1-quart casserole. Add one-third of the crumbs and press them firmly into an even layer on bottom and sides of dish. Spoon one-half of the applesauce into the dish. Dot with one-half the remaining butter and sprinkle with one-half the remaining crumbs. Repeat layering, ending with crumbs.
3. Bake at 350°F 30 to 40 minutes, or until crumbs are golden brown.
4. Cool completely and chill.
5. To form a design on top of cake, sift confectioners' sugar through a lacy paper doily placed on cake, then carefully lift off doily.
6. For vanilla sauce, cream butter and sugar thoroughly.
7. Add egg yolks gradually, beating constantly until fluffy.
8. Stir in boiling water very gradually. Pour mixture into the top of a double boiler. Cook over simmering water, stirring until thickened. Blend in vanilla extract. Cool; chill in refrigerator.

8 servings

DECEMBER
Holiday Parties

Giving a party is always something of a juggling act. There is only so much time and too many things to do. The hostess who manages to get everything done has probably learned the trick of doing two things at once. In December, she is apt to schedule a party to coincide with something else she wants to do—tree trimming, caroling, or sledding.

Try putting her method to work for your own December party. If you follow through on the principle of making your efforts do double duty, you won't need to think up an activity. Just bring the gang home after a holiday outing or let them help trim the tree. This sort of party has appeal for all ages, so consider extending invitations to whole families rather than just to the grownups.

FOOD

Since it's in season, turn to traditional holiday food. If your activity takes you outdoors plan to serve a warm drink when you return. It is, literally, the best icebreaker.

In the alcoholic category, seasonal favorites are mulled wine, burgundy bishop, and glögg. And don't overlook the nonalcoholic warmers, especially if you're including the little ones. Steaming cocoa topped with melting marshmallows is a universal hit, but if you want to go fancier, serve French chocolate.

Russian tea is good, too, and easy to do. Make the mix in advance and just add boiling water at serving time. Since this recipe makes a large quantity, you could tie up little packets of the dry mixture for take-home gifts for the guests.

Coffeehouses offer a variety of coffee combinations you could try, everything from café au lait for the non-drinkers to Irish coffee for the rest.

Chances are you'll be making fruitcakes for gifts. Let your baking serve two purposes and make extra cakes for your December party. The same goes for the cookies you're sure to make for teachers, Scout leaders, and neighbors.

Generally, it's not a good idea to double recipes for baked goods but you can still save time by doing the collecting, chopping, measuring of ingredients all on the same day. Bake several single batches, one at a time, and cleanup will be little more trouble than for one batch.

DECORATIONS

Like decorations for the New Year's open house, these will be traditional items you'll display for the family's observance of the season. Another good example of doing two things at once!

A crackling log in the fireplace and some seasonal music, preferably sung by a group around the piano, will create the right framework for holiday socializing. And with forethought you can put yourself into the picture, enjoying the party along with your guests.

BEVERAGES

Burgundy Bishop

2 oranges
1 lemon
2 cups water
½ cup sugar
10 whole cloves
6 whole allspice
2 sticks (3 inches each) cinnamon
2 bottles (⁴/₅ quart each) Burgundy, chilled

1. Slice oranges and lemon. Set aside slices of one orange for garnish.
2. Boil slices in water with sugar, cloves, allspice, and cinnamon. Strain. Cool.
3. Add to chilled Burgundy; serve cold.
4. Garnish the punch bowl and cups with **fresh orange slices** studded with **cloves.**

About 1½ quarts

Mulled Wine

1½ cups water
1 cup sugar
3 lemons, sliced
3 sticks cinnamon
3 tablespoons whole cloves
3 bottles (⁴/₅ quart each) dry red wine
1 can (46 ounces) pineapple juice
2 cans (6 ounces each) frozen orange juice concentrate, reconstituted as directed

1. Boil water with sugar, lemon, and spices for 5 minutes.
2. Strain; mix with wine, pineapple juice, and orange juice. Heat through; do not boil. Serve hot.

42 half-cup servings

Glögg

1 bottle (25 ounces) Aquavit
1 bottle (25 ounces) claret
1 cup (about 5 ounces) blanched almonds
6 (2½-inch) cinnamon sticks
1 cup (about 4 ounces) dark seedless raisins
6 pieces candied orange or lemon peel
12 whole cloves
12 cardamom seeds, peeled
1 cup loaf sugar

1. Combine Aquavit and claret in a large saucepan or saucepot. Add the almonds, cinnamon sticks, raisins, orange peel, cloves, and cardamom seeds to mixture. Bring slowly to boiling. Reduce heat and simmer 10 minutes. Remove saucepan from heat.
2. Put 1 cup loaf sugar in large sieve and place over saucepan. Using a ladle or large spoon, pour some of the mixture from the saucepan over the sugar. Ignite the sugar with a match. Continue to pour the liquid over the sugar until the sugar has completely melted. The liquid will be flaming. If necessary, extinguish flame by placing cover over saucepan.
3. Serve Glögg hot in mugs or punch glasses. Be sure there are some raisins and almonds in each portion.

10 to 15 servings

DECEMBER—HOLIDAY PARTIES

Russian Spiced Tea Mix

1 jar (9 ounces) orange-flavored instant breakfast drink
½ to 1 cup instant tea
½ to 1 cup sugar
1 teaspoon ground cinnamon
½ teaspoon ground cloves

1. Mix all ingredients well. Store in tightly covered container.
2. At serving time, use 2 to 3 heaping teaspoons to 1 cup of boiling water.

About 4 cups tea mix

Black Coffee (Café Noir)

2 to 4 tablespoons drip grind coffee (depending upon strength desired)

1. Preheat a drip coffee maker by filling it with boiling water. Drain.
2. For each standard measuring cup of water, using standard measuring spoon, measure coffee. Put into filter section of drip coffee maker.
3. Bring water to boiling. Measure and pour boiling water into upper container, about 2 tablespoons at a time. Cover. Allow all of the water to drip through the coffee. Repeat the small additions of boiling water. After 4 or 5 additions of water have been made, set coffee maker over very low heat while coffee is dripping. Repeat additions of water until desired quantity of coffee is made. Do not let coffee boil at any time.
4. Remove coffee compartment; stir and cover the brew. If coffee cannot be served immediately, let stand over low heat without boiling.

Note: For Café au Lait, add ½ cup scalded milk or cream to ½ cup Black Coffee; simultaneously pour hot coffee and hot milk into cup. Sweeten, if desired.

Irish Coffee

1½ ounces Irish whiskey
Hot black coffee
Sugar to taste
Softly whipped cream

1. Prewarm a 7-ounce goblet.
2. Pour in Irish whiskey and add coffee to within a half inch of the top. Add sugar and stir.
3. Carefully float whipped cream on top. Sip drink through the cream.

1 serving

Hot Chocolate

2 ounces (2 squares) unsweetened chocolate
¾ cup water
5 to 6 tablespoons sugar
⅛ teaspoon salt
3¼ cups milk
1 teaspoon vanilla extract

1. In a saucepan combine chocolate, water, sugar, and salt and cook over low heat, stirring constantly.
2. When chocolate is melted, increase heat and boil 3 minutes, stirring constantly. Reduce heat, add milk gradually, and heat to scalding; do not boil. Stir in vanilla extract.

6 servings

French Chocolate

- 1 square (1 ounce) unsweetened chocolate
- ½ cup water
- 6 tablespoons sugar
- Dash of salt
- ¼ cup whipping cream, whipped
- 2 cups hot milk

1. Put chocolate, water, sugar, and salt into a saucepan, and stir over low heat until well blended. Cook for 10 minutes, stirring so that the mixture does not scorch.
2. Cool. Fold in the whipped cream.
3. To serve, spoon some of the chocolate cream into each cup and pour in the hot milk.

3 servings

FRUITCAKES

Brownie Fruitcake

- 1½ cups walnuts (7 ounces)
- 1 cup halved candied cherries (8 ounces)
- 1 cup diced mixed candied fruits (8 ounces)
- 1 cup sliced dates (5 ounces)
- ½ cup hot coffee
- ¼ cup unsweetened cocoa
- 1¾ cups sifted all-purpose flour
- ¼ teaspoon baking soda
- ¾ teaspoon salt
- ¼ teaspoon cinnamon
- ⅛ teaspoon cloves
- ½ cup butter or margarine
- 1 teaspoon vanilla extract
- 1¼ cups packed brown sugar
- 2 eggs
- 4 to 6 walnut halves
- Candied cherry halves
- Angelica, citron, or candied pineapple strips

1. Chop walnuts coarsely; combine with candied fruits and dates.
2. Stir coffee and cocoa together; set aside to cool.
3. Line bottom and sides of an 11×4½×2¾-inch loaf pan with one thickness of greased brown paper and one of greased waxed paper, allowing paper to extend about 1 inch above sides and ends of pan.
4. Sift flour with baking soda, salt, and spices.
5. Cream butter, vanilla extract, and brown sugar well. Add eggs, one at a time, beating thoroughly after each addition (mixture will look curdled). Blend in flour mixture alternately with cocoa mixture. Stir in chopped walnuts and fruits. Turn into prepared pan. Arrange walnut halves on top.
6. Place a shallow pan of hot water on oven floor. Set filled loaf pan on lowest rack of oven. Put a piece of brown paper on paper lining pan.
7. Bake at 300°F 2 to 2¼ hours, or until cake tests done. Cool in pan.
8. To decorate, arrange cherry halves and angelica strips between walnut halves.

One 3¾-pound fruitcake

White Walnut Fruitcake

- 1½ cups walnuts (7 ounces)
- 1½ cups halved candied cherries (12 ounces)
- 1 cup diced candied pineapple (6 ounces)
- ¾ cup diced candied orange peel (4 ounces)
- ¾ cup diced candied lemon peel (4 ounces)
- ¾ cup diced citron (4 ounces)
- ¾ cup brandy
- 2 cups sifted all-purpose flour

1. Chop walnuts coarsely and set aside.
2. Combine candied fruits and peels in a bowl. Pour ½ cup brandy over fruit, stir to moisten, cover, and let stand several hours or overnight.
3. Line bottom and sides of a 9-inch tube pan with one thickness of greased brown paper and one of greased waxed paper.
4. Sift flour with baking powder, salt, and mace.
5. Cream butter and sugar until light and fluffy. Beat in egg yolks and grated peel. Add dry ingredients alternately with remaining ¼ cup brandy to creamed mixture, mixing well after each addition. Mix in walnuts and brandied fruit.

DECEMBER—HOLIDAY PARTIES

- ¾ teaspoon baking powder
- 1 teaspoon salt
- 1 teaspoon mace
- ¾ cup butter or margarine
- 1 cup sugar
- 4 eggs, separated
- 1 tablespoon grated orange peel
- ½ teaspoon cream of tartar
- Confectioners' sugar
- Angelica or citron strips
- Candied cherries

6. Beat egg whites with cream of tartar until stiff, not dry, peaks are formed. Fold into fruit mixture. Spoon into prepared pan and spread level.
7. Place a shallow pan of hot water on oven floor. Set filled tube pan on lowest rack of oven.
8. Bake at 300°F about 2½ hours, or until cake tests done. Cool cake in pan.
9. To decorate, sift confectioners' sugar lightly over top of cake. Decorate with strips of angelica or citron and candied cherries.

One 4½-pound fruitcake

Irish Fruitcake

- 1½ cups walnuts (7 ounces)
- ¾ cup dark seedless raisins (4 ounces)
- ¾ cup golden raisins (4 ounces)
- ¾ cup currants (3 ounces)
- ¾ cup diced citron (4 ounces)
- ¾ cup diced candied orange peel (4 ounces)
- ¾ cup halved candied cherries (6 ounces)
- ½ cup Irish whiskey or bourbon
- 1 tablespoon molasses
- 1 teaspoon grated lemon peel
- 2 cups sifted all-purpose flour
- ½ teaspoon baking powder
- 1 teaspoon salt
- 1 teaspoon cinnamon
- ½ teaspoon nutmeg
- ½ teaspoon allspice
- ¾ cup butter or margarine
- 1 cup packed brown sugar
- 3 eggs
- Confectioners' sugar
- Water
- Green food coloring
- Green decorator sugar
- Walnut halves

1. Chop walnuts coarsely and set aside.
2. Combine raisins, currants, and candied fruits and peels with ⅓ cup whiskey, molasses, and lemon peel. Mix well, cover, and let stand overnight.
3. The next day, sift flour with baking powder, salt, and spices.
4. Cream butter and brown sugar well. Add eggs, one at a time, beating thoroughly after each addition (mixture will look curdled). Blend flour mixture into creamed mixture. Add fruits and walnuts and mix well.
5. Turn into a well-greased 9-inch Bundt pan.
6. Place a shallow pan of hot water on oven floor. Set filled Bundt pan on lowest rack of oven.
7. Bake at 300°F about 1¾ hours, or until cake tests done. Let cool 10 minutes in pan, then invert cake onto wire rack and spoon remaining whiskey slowly over cake so it soaks in. Cool cake completely.
8. To decorate, mix a small amount of confectioners' sugar with enough water to thin to pouring consistency. Tint lightly with food coloring; drizzle over top of cake. Sprinkle with green sugar and arrange walnut halves on top.

One 3¾-pound fruitcake

Banana Walnut Fruitcake

- 1½ cups walnuts (7 ounces)
- 2 cups mixed candied fruits (1 pound)
- 1¾ cups sifted all-purpose flour
- 1 teaspoon baking powder
- ¼ teaspoon baking soda
- 1 teaspoon salt
- ¼ teaspoon nutmeg
- ⅔ cup butter or margarine
- ¾ cup sugar
- 2 eggs
- 1 cup mashed banana (3 small bananas)
- Confectioners' sugar (optional)

1. Chop walnuts coarsely. Chop candied fruits finely and combine with walnuts in a bowl; set aside.
2. Sift flour with baking powder, baking soda, salt, and nutmeg.
3. Cream butter and sugar well. Add eggs, one at a time, beating thoroughly after each addition. Blend in flour mixture alternately with mashed banana.
4. Pour batter over fruit-walnut mixture and blend well.
5. Turn into a well-greased tube pan (about 2-quart capacity).
6. Place a shallow pan of hot water on oven floor. Set filled tube pan on lowest rack of oven.
7. Bake at 300°F about 1¼ hours, or until a wooden pick inserted in center comes out clean and dry. Cool 15 minutes in pan, then invert cake onto wire rack to cool.
8. Serve plain or with a light sifting of confectioners' sugar.

One 3-pound fruitcake

Double Walnut Fruitcake

- 2½ cups walnuts (12 ounces)
- 1 cup candied pineapple chunks (6 ounces)
- 1 cup halved candied cherries (8 ounces)
- 1 cup sliced dates (5 ounces)
- ½ cup golden raisins (3 ounces)
- 1½ cups sifted all-purpose flour
- 1 teaspoon baking powder
- 1 teaspoon salt
- ⅔ cup butter or margarine
- 1 teaspoon vanilla extract
- 1 cup packed brown sugar
- 3 eggs
- Confectioners' sugar
- Water
- Mixed candied fruits and peels

1. Chop 1 cup walnuts coarsely; combine with candied fruits, dates, and raisins.
2. Grate remaining 1½ cups walnuts with Mouli grater (or put into an electric blender, ¼ cup at a time, and blend to a fine meal).
3. Sift flour with baking powder and salt.
4. Cream butter, vanilla extract, and brown sugar well. Add eggs, one at a time, beating thoroughly after each addition (mixture will look curdled). Blend in flour mixture and grated walnuts. Mix in walnut-fruit mixture.
5. Turn into a well-greased 11×4½×2¾-inch loaf pan or other pan with 2-quart capacity.
6. Place a shallow pan of hot water on oven floor. Set filled loaf pan on lowest rack of oven.
7. Bake at 300°F about 2 hours, or until cake tests done. Cool in pan 30 minutes, then turn cake out onto wire rack to cool.
8. To decorate, mix a little confectioners' sugar with enough water to thin to pouring consistency. Drizzle over top of cake. Pile candied fruits down center.

One 3½-pound fruitcake

COOKIES

Noel Cookies

- 1 cup butter, softened
- 1 cup firmly packed dark brown sugar
- 3 eggs
- 3 cups sifted all-purpose flour
- 1 teaspoon baking soda

1. Cream butter and brown sugar. Add eggs, one at a time, beating well after each.
2. Sift flour, baking soda, and cinnamon together; alternately add with milk to creamed mixture, beating until blended after each addition. Add sherry, walnuts, and fruits; mix well.

DECEMBER—HOLIDAY PARTIES

1 teaspoon cinnamon
½ cup milk
2 tablespoons sherry
7 cups chopped walnuts
1 cup chopped candied pineapple
2 cups candied cherries (1 cup red and 1 cup green), chopped
2 cups chopped dates
¾ pound golden raisins
Candied cherries for decoration

3. Drop by teaspoonfuls onto greased cookie sheets. Decorate with candied cherry pieces.
4. Bake at 300°F about 20 minutes. Cool cookies on racks.

About 14 dozen cookies

Holiday Wreaths

1 cup butter or margarine
1 package (3 ounces) cream cheese
1 cup sugar
1 egg yolk
1 teaspoon vanilla extract
2¾ cups all-purpose flour
¼ teaspoon baking powder
Green and red decorator sugar

1. Cream butter, cream cheese, and sugar. Add egg yolk and vanilla extract; beat well. Blend flour and baking powder; mix into creamed mixture.
2. Press dough through a cookie press, using wreath design disc, onto ungreased cookie sheets. Decorate with sugar.
3. Bake at 350°F 10 to 15 minutes, or until very pale brown around edges; do not overbake. Cool cookies on wire racks.

About 8 dozen cookies

CANDY

English Toffee

1 pound butter or margarine
2 tablespoons water
2 cups sugar
½ teaspoon salt
2 cups finely chopped walnuts
10 ounces milk chocolate

1. Butter a 14×10-inch pan.
2. Melt butter with water in a heavy 10- to 12-inch skillet over medium-high heat. Add sugar and salt, stirring constantly with a wooden spoon. Bring to boiling; if using a candy thermometer, set in place. Cook until the boiling mixture begins to lose its yellow color and takes a whitish look. Mix in 1 cup chopped walnuts. Continue cooking and stirring until toffee is a caramel color (298° to 300°F). Turn mixture into buttered pan and cool slightly. Mark into squares with a sharp knife. Cool.
3. Melt chocolate in a double boiler over hot, not steaming, water.
4. Spread chocolate over cooled toffee. Sprinkle with remaining walnuts. Let stand until chocolate is set. Break toffee into pieces.

About 3 pounds toffee

INDEX

Appetizers
  angels on horseback (England), 82
  appetizer party pie, 25
  blue cheese dip with vegetable strips, 12
  chicken liver pâté, 12
  clam and walnut stuffed mushrooms, 12
  empanadas (Chile), 83
  gala pecan spread, 24
  mock caviar (eggplant), 12
  mushroom cheese mold, 11
  mushrooms à la grecque, 11
  Swedish lemon meatballs, 25
April—Bachelor's Brunch
  brunch, bachelor style, 35
  Gerry's brunch, 32
  invitations, 31
  menu, 31
  spring tonic brunch, 34
August—Posh Picnics
  before the concert affair, 64
  menu, 61
  midsummer night scene, 66
  table setting, 62
  timing, 62
  wine, 62
  wine tasting picnic, 62

Barbecue(d)
  basics, 56–57
  beef chuck steak, 54
  getting ready to barbecue, 54
  sauces, 55, 59–60
Beef
  barbecue basics
    burgers, 56
    kabobs, 56
    rib roast, 56
    steaks, 56
  burger loaf, marinated onion-topped, 55
  chuck steak, barbecued, 54
  'n' buns, saucy, 68
Beverages
  apple ice, 38
  black coffee (café noir), 89
  bloody Mary, 35
  Burgundy bishop, 88
  café au lait, 89
  café noir, 89
  champagne punch, 10
  cranberry ice, 38
  French chocolate, 90
  gin punch, 10
  glögg, 88
  hot chocolate, 89
  Irish coffee, 89
  mulled wine, 88
  Russian spiced tea mix, 89
  silver gin fizz, 32
  spring tonic, 34
  strawberry punch, 10
  Thanksgiving wine bowl, 80
Black-eyed devils, 33
Bread
  garlic, 58
  zucchini, 65
Brownies, see Desserts

Cakes, see Desserts
Canadian bacon rolls, barbecue basics, 56
Chicken
  -almond sandwich filling, 69
  barbecue basics, 57
  fiesta buns, 70
  liver pâté, 12
  livers in wild rice ring, 34
  mousse, 42
  salad Polynesian, 41
Chili dogs, 75
Cookies, see Desserts
Crab meat mousse, 66
Crepes, salmon quiche, 35

December—Holiday Parties
  beverages, 88–90
  candy, 93
  cookies, 92–93
  decorations, 87
  food, 87
  fruitcakes, 90–92
Decorations
  December—Holiday Parties, 87
  January—Open House, 10
  July—Cookout, 53
  November—Melting Potluck, planning, 80
  table
    for grade schoolers, 18
    for preschoolers, 18
Desserts
  applecake with vanilla sauce (Sweden), 86
  bananas Foster Brennan's, 30
  blueberry cookie tarts, 72
  blueberry lattice-top pie, 71
  brownies
    blonde, 77
    mallow-nut, 77
  cakes
    angel food spice, 50
    choo-choo, 20
    farmer's Sunday (Ireland), 86
    jack-o-lantern, 76
    nectarine chiffon, 49
    sherry-coconut chiffon, 63
    sweetheart, 21
    triple chocolate, 50
  cherry flambée, 30
  chocolate-banana frozen pops, 22
  chocolate fondue, 30
  cookies
    filbert drops, 72
    French lemon bars, 44
    holiday wreaths, 93
    Noel, 92
    pumpkin jumbos, 78
    squares, double quick, 22
  light plum pudding, 16
  peach puffs, 72
  peppermint stick charlotte, 29
  pineapple cream filling, 22
  very blueberry pie, 71
Dip(s)
  blue cheese, with vegetable strips, 12
  cottage cheese, 70
  special blender cheese, 76
  tempting tuna, 21
Duck, barbecue basics, 57

Empanadas (Chile), 83

February—Children's Parties
  grade schoolers
    food, 19
    games, 18
    party theme, 18
    table decorations, 18
    Valentine party, 20
  preschoolers
    food, 18
    games, 17
    parties for, 17
    party theme, 17
    table decorations, 18
    train party for, 19
Fettuccine al burro Alfredo (Italy), 84
Filbert drops, 72
Filling(s)
  celery-olive, 39
  pineapple cream, 22
  sandwich
    chicken-almond, 69
    creamy ham, 69
    sliced tomato, 69
  shrimp, 39
  zippy cheese, 39
Fish, see specific kinds
Fondue, chocolate, 30
Frankfurters
  barbecue basics, 56
  chili dogs, 75
  silly dogs, 19
  taco dogs, 74

INDEX

French dressings, *see* Salad dressings
Frosting(s)
  creamy chocolate, 51
  creamy orange, 78
  jack-o-lantern, 76
  lemon butter, 86
  seven-minute, 22
  sharp cheese, 69
Fruit
  apples in foil, baked, 58
  avocado and grapefruit segments on bibb lettuce, 36
  bananas Foster Brennan's, 30
  candied cranberries, 81
  cherry flambée, 30
  chocolate-banana frozen pops, 22
  cottage cheese-melon mold, 41
  grapes, herbed carrots with, 14
  overnight cherry salad, 15
  salad, frozen, 38
  shrimp and avocado salad, 42
  smorgasbord pear salads, 39
Fruitcake
  banana walnut, 92
  brownie, 90
  double walnut, 92
  Irish, 91
  white walnut, 90

Games
  for grade schoolers, 18
  for preschoolers, 17
Giblets and broth, cooked, 81

Ham
  creamy sandwich filling, 69
  glazed smoked, 13
  loaf in a jacket, 62
  slices, barbecue basics, 56

Ice cream
  banana, 49
  berry, 47
  buttered pecan, 47
  cherry jubilee, 48
  chocolate, 47
  chocolate chip, 47
  favorite vanilla, 46
  freezer chocolate, 48
  French vanilla, 46
  making, 45–46
  nectarine ripple, 47
  peach, 47
  Philadelphia, 49
  sauces, 51–52
  social, 45
  strawberry, 49

January—Open House
  appetizers, 11–12
  beverages, 10
  decorations, 10
  desserts, 16
  invitations, 9
  meat dishes, 13
  salad molds, 15–16
  vegetables, 14
  what to serve, 9
July—Cookout
  barbecue basics, 56–57
  decorations, 53
  food, 53
  getting ready to barbecue, 54
  main dishes, 54–55
  sauces and accompaniments, 55, 59–60
  side dishes from the grill, 58
June—Ice Cream Social
  cakes, 49–50
  ice cream
    making, 45–46
    recipes, 46–49
    sauces, 51–52
  menu, 45

Kabobs
  beef, barbecue basics, 56
  lamb, barbecue basics, 56

Lamb
  barbecue basics
    kabobs, 56
    loin chops, 56
    patties, 57
    rib chops, 56
    shoulder chops, 56
  roast leg of, French style, 28
Lasagne, turkey, 13
Liver(s)
  chicken, in wild rice ring, 34
  pâté, chicken, 12
Lobster, barbecue basics
  live, 57
  rock lobster tails, 57

Macaroni salad, all-seasons, 41
March—Progressive Dinner Party
  appetizers, 24–25
  continental cuisine, 27
  dessert course, 24
  desserts, 29–30
  French dinner, 28
  fruit and cheese course, 24
  Greek dinner, 26
  hospitality hour, 23
  how to organize, 23
  main course, 24
  salad course, 24
Marshmallows, toasted, 58
May—Bridal Showers
  activities, 38
  guest list, 37
  invitations, 37
  menu, 37
  recipes for, 38–44
  salad bar, 37
  salad buffet, 37
Meatballs, Swedish lemon, 25
Menus
  before the concert affair, 64
  brunch, bachelor style, 35
  continental cuisine, 27
  French dinner, 28
  Gerry's brunch, 32
  grade schooler's Valentine party, 20
  Greek dinner, 26
  melting potluck dinner party, 82
  midsummer night scene, 66
  spring tonic brunch, 34
  traditional Thanksgiving dinner, 80
  train party for preschoolers, 19
  wine tasting picnic, 62
Mold(s)
  chicken livers in wild rice ring, 34
  cottage cheese-melon, 41
  mushroom-cheese, 11
Mousse
  artichoke, 15
  chicken, 42
  crab meat, 66

Noodles, creamy green, 28
November—Melting Potluck
  giving the party, 80
  melting potluck dinner party, 82
  planning decorations, 80
  planning the food, 79
  traditional Thanksgiving dinner, 80

October—Teen Party
  activities, 73
  food, 73
  recipes for, 74–78

Party theme(s)
  for grade schoolers, 18
  for preschoolers, 17
Pastitsio (Greek pasta casserole), 26
Pâté, chicken liver, 12
Pies, *see* Desserts
Pizza loaf, salami, 75
Popcorn or balls, caramel, 77
Pork
  barbecue basics
    Canadian bacon roll, 56
    franks, 56
    ham slices, 56
    smoked shoulder roll, 56
    spareribs, 56

96 INDEX

sauce-painted spareribs, 54
Poultry, see specific kinds
Puddings, see Desserts
Punches, see Beverages

Ratatouille (France), 85
Ratatouille in packets, 58
Relish, onion confetti, 60
Rice
    chicken livers in wild rice ring, 34
    Mexican, 84
    soubise, 28
Rock Cornish hen, barbecue basics, 57

Salad(s)
    all-seasons macaroni, 41
    bar, 37
    buffet, 37
    chicken, Polynesian, 41
    frozen fruit, 38
    Greek, 26
    hot potato (Germany), 85
    layered overnight, 40
    Polish tomato, 85
    Roquefort-vegetable, 65
    salade Niçoise, 40
    salade Provençale, 29
    shrimp and avocado, 42
    smorgasbord pear, 39
    spinach mushroom, 33
Salad dressing(s)
    celery seed, 36
    cooked pineapple, 16
    creamy lemon-celery seed, 44
    French
        creamy, 43
        curried, 43
        honey, 43
        honey-lime, 43
        Lorenzo, 43
        tangy, 43
        tomato soup, 43
    green goddess, 44
    pineapple, 39
    Roquefort cheese, 43

Salad mold(s)
    artichoke mousse, 15
    overnight cherry salad, 15
    party perfect, 21
    potato salad, 42
Salami pizza loaf, 75
Salmon
    glazed decorated, 64
    quiche crepes, 35
Sandwich(es)
    chicken fiesta buns, 70
    fillings, 69
    loaf, golden frosted, 69
    mushroom-sauced, 71
    Roquefort-tongue, 68
    saucy beef 'n' buns, 68
    super, 68
Sauce(s)
    butter, 59
    butterscotch, 51
    chocolate fudge, 51
    hard, 16
    herb barbecue, 59
    lemon, 52
    lemon barbecue, 59
    nectarine-pineapple sundae, 51
    orange butter, 59
    peppy barbecue, 55
    savory onion topper, 60
    strawberry, 52
    sweet-sour apricot, 60
    vanilla, 52, 86
    walnut praline, 52
September—Card Parties
    ladies' night out, 67, 69
    male call, 68
    male call card party, 67
    mixed couples' card party, 68, 71
Shrimp
    and avocado salad, 42
    barbecue basics, 57
Side Dishes from the Grill, 58
Snack mix, 74
Soufflé Mont Blanc, 65
Spareribs
    barbecue basics, 56
    sauce-painted, 54

Spread(s)
    gala pecan, 24
    mock caviar (eggplant), 12
    mushroom cheese, 11

Taco dogs, 74
Taffy, brown sugar, 75
Toffee, English, 93
Tongue sandwich, Roquefort-, 68
Tuna
    dip, tempting, 21
    pie, topsy-turvy, 33
Turkey
    barbecue basics, 57
    lasagne, 13
    roast, 81

Valentine party, grade schoolers', 20
Veal
    carbonada criolla (Argentina), 84
    epicurean, 27
    steak cordon bleu (Switzerland), 83
Vegetables
    asparagus vinaigrette, 27
    beans, sweet-sour, in tomato shells, 66
    carrots, herbed, with grapes, 14
    corn, roast, 58
    green pepper shells, 70
    mushrooms à la grecque, 11
    mushrooms, clam and walnut stuffed, 12
    onion rings, crispy french-fried, 60
    onions, grilled, 58
    potatoes, baked, 58
    potatoes, make-ahead mashed, 14
    ratatouille (France), 85
    ratatouille in packets, 58
    Roquefort-vegetable salad, 65
    spinach-cheese bake, 14
    spinach, Hungarian creamed, 85
    strips, with blue cheese dip, 12
    tomatoes, grilled, 58
    tomato shells, 70